Racing on the Edge
Season 2003

		page
Preface		**5**
Inside BMW	Flying start	**10**
GP Australia	Lap by Lap	**16**
	Revolution from above	**20**
GP Malaysia	Lap by Lap	**22**
	The first time	**26**
GP Brazil	Lap by Lap	**28**
	Happiness after the hard work	**32**
Inside BMW	A silent goodbye	**34**
GP San Marino	Lap by Lap	**40**
	The last victory of the Red Goddess	**44**
GP Spain	Lap by Lap	**46**
	At the height of fashion	**50**
GP Austria	Lap by Lap	**52**
	Felix Austria	**56**
Inside BMW	The turbo party	**58**
GP Monaco	Lap by Lap	**66**
	Light at the end of the tunnel	**70**
GP Canada	Lap by Lap	**74**
	Always neatly in line	**78**
GP Europe	Lap by Lap	**80**
	The double victory	**84**
Inside BMW	"The challenge remains..."	**92**
GP France	Lap by Lap	**98**
	From 0 to 100 km/h	**102**
GP Great Britain	Lap by Lap	**104**
	The dolphin dives	**108**
GP Germany	Lap by Lap	**110**
	The television court is in session	**114**
Inside BMW	Up, up and away	**116**
GP Hungary	Lap by Lap	**122**
	Alonso, the youngest...	**126**
GP Italy	Lap by Lap	**128**
	The substitute	**132**
Inside BMW	The tyre test	**134**
GP USA	Lap by Lap	**140**
	The hard plight of the men at Sauber	**144**
GP Japan	Lap by Lap	**146**
	Bad race, good season	**150**
	Statistics	**158**

contents

Dear reader,

Who would have thought it? What appeared to be complete dominance by Ferrari at the start of the year actually developed into the most exciting season we've had for years.

The 16 races in the 2003 season were won by no fewer than eight different drivers from five different teams. Shortly before the season ended, three teams had a realistic chance of taking the title. For me, this is evidence of the high degree of expertise contained in the minds and the cars. Furthermore, this is certainly a guarantee for spectators that things will continue to be exciting for seasons to come.

The 2003 season has been a demonstration of just how the tide can turn, and that many more factors, other than the driver and technology have a role to play in Formula One. Towards the end of the season, however, our team ultimately lacked a little of the luck required to defend our points lead in the constructors' championship.

On behalf of the entire Board of BMW AG, I would like to congratulate our team in Munich and Grove, as well as both our drivers, on this season's outstanding results. With four victories, including two one-two finishes in succession, this has been our greatest season so far. The team achieved an exceptional second place behind Ferrari and ahead of McLaren Mercedes. In the drivers' championship, our drivers, Juan Pablo Montoya and Ralf Schumacher, finished the season in third and fifth positions respectively at the top of the table.

I am particularly pleased with the constantly high level of performance and reliability: Our two drivers completed the highest number of laps this year, which demonstrates the extraordinary reliability of the FW25 and the P83 engine. This reflects the efficient quality management in the entire development process in Grove and in Munich.

As I write, the technical preparations for next year's engine are already in full swing. Following successful test bench runs, the P84 engine was put to the test at the Monza track at the start of September.

I am certain – not least because of the remarkably positive initial feedback from the Monza test – that we will generate further excitement and be a top player once again in the 2004 season.

I hope you enjoy reading this book.

Best regards,

Prof Dr Burkhard Göschel

Welcome

Flying start

The media want facts and a fantastic show. The technicians want to work. And the BMW WilliamsF1 Team wants to do the right thing by both sides.

Just how do you get a refuelling nozzle to not pump fuel, but instead to suck up a wafer-thin silk cloth and unveil the WilliamsF1 BMW FW25 to the world public for the first time? This is typical of the tasks required for an official car launch in racing's elite division. What has not the sector done in its pursuit of arousing admiration: Holiday on Ice, Cats, Sicilian open-air theatres, Planet Hollywood, Hard Rock Café – for many teams, no equipment or location is too extravagant or too unusual in the quest to bring their new cars and corresponding sponsors the level of attention which befits them.

In doing so, every team presentation is faced with a dilemma: On the one hand, the team, car and sponsors deserve the best possible presentation. On the other hand, the team, car and sponsors would also benefit from axing this presentation altogether due to time constraints.

Formula One is a permanent battle against time. During every race, before every race – even before the season begins. Only 145 days of preparation separate the last lap of the Suzuka race marking the end of the season and the roars of the engines at the inaugural race of the new season in Melbourne. Every day which is not invested in developing the new car causes great pain.

This is without even mentioning the three days which, according to BMW Track Operation Manager Franz Tost, can be taken up by the team presentation: "The type of team presentation known jokingly in the industry as the 'musical production' costs valuable development time. One day for taking the car to the presentation, one day for the presentation itself and at least another day – if not more – for the journey on to the test track."

Three days on the move equate to three days of stagnation. It is a luxury which a first-rate team cannot afford. Franz Tost is certain of the fact: "Fortunately at BMW WilliamsF1 Team, an approach is taken to ensure that no time is lost. The car is showcased to the public for an hour at the track, then it is towed into the garage to allow the testing to begin. This satisfies everyone: The media get their pictures and a story, and the team are able to start their work on the same day."

This may sound simple, but in fact it requires meticulous preparation. Responsibility for this preparation at BMW lies in the hands of the Motorsport Technology and Communications Department, which also provides early answers to crucial questions in agreement with WilliamsF1. Which is the best day in January for the presentation? At which circuit can free image material be produced whilst taking media law into consideration? Which circuit can offer a certain climatic reliability? This last question still needs to be rephrased, since it automatically excludes Silverstone – even if this circuit would otherwise be ideal due to the short distance to the WilliamsF1 headquarters in Grove. No, nobody wants a snow-covered Silverstone – in fact, the only suitable place in Europe during the winter is Spain. Jerez, Valencia, Barcelona. The latter can most easily be integrated into the normal testing schedule – Barcelona it is then!

Once the location has been decided, the question now concerns the style of the presentation. Together, BMW and WilliamsF1 consider various alternatives. Jaguar, one of the competitors, attempted an entirely virtual presentation on the internet for the first time in 2003. It was certainly worth trying, but can an internet presentation – no matter how good – really replace the face-to-face interaction between the media and the protagonists? At BMW and their partner WilliamsF1, one thing is for sure: "We want direct contact between jounalists and team members and the interview opportunities that this brings." Direct contact means many people. 450 journalists from all over the world are invited and want to be part of the action at the presentation held at the Circuit de Catalunya, and then there are sponsors on top of that. In addition to providing work stations, appropriate hospitality is also expected. First of all, a representatives' marquee must be provided – but not just any marquee, because it can be extremely windy in Barcelona. For BMW, this occasion is the time to obtain tenders from event agencies, which are given a few specific tasks to complete as part of the tendering process. Owing to the sheer number of photographers with different viewpoints, the new WilliamsF1 BMW FW25 must be showcased on a rotatable stage. In the background, all the partition walls must be arranged in such a way as to enable each BMW WilliamsF1 Team sponsor to get their money's worth. The wait now begins for tenders from the events agencies to be received.

Meanwhile, the internal exchange between BMW Technology and Communication and WilliamsF1 continues. A telephone conference is held to discuss which of the main players should be on the stage during the car launch. Should the partition walls only display the team logo, or should all the other sponsors be displayed? If the other sponsors are to appear, which colours should be used and how large should they be?

The invitation procedure involves a protracted selection process and a great deal of organisation. Who is to be invited from the media? Who needs a hotel? Are hostesses available in the hotels to serve as

contact persons? Who needs a shuttle service from the airport to the hotel? Who needs to be taken from the hotel to the circuit? And who needs transport from the circuit to the airport? Are the meeting points at the airport clearly signposted? And so on and so forth …

The event agency and BMW have their hands full. In conjunction with BMW Spain, the fleet of 7 series and 5 series vehicles and their drivers is organised. Naturally, BMW Technology and Communication pays particular attention to the equipment in the press centre. 140 seats are planned, in addition to 40 computers from the sponsor HP, and just as many telephone points – both analogue and ISDN.

The staging of the presentation is planned meticulously. The compère, Jonathan Legard, will welcome all the attendees. He is on the stage together with the team's main players: Sir Frank Williams, Patrick Head, Dr Mario Theissen, Gerhard Berger, chief technicians Gavin Fisher and Sam Michael, as well as the drivers Ralf Schumacher, Juan Pablo Montoya and Marc Gené. Legard will direct the first questions at these people and integrate them into a dialogue.

Once the stage presentation is over, the four interview corners become the focus of interest. One corner is for German-speaking journalists, another corner is for their English-speaking colleagues, a third corner is for people from other countries and the fourth corner is reserved for the television crews. Once all the questions have been asked, all pictures taken and all film footage shot, everything is available at the marquee exit: Approximately 400 bags containing press packs for the 2003 season, in English and German.

If everything goes according to plan, the journalists are likely to hear the loud noise of the BMW P83 engine: The time for the inaugural run of the brand-new WilliamsF1 BMW FW25 has now arrived. The concept of this special presentation reveals its success at this moment, i.e. transforming the time constraint into a virtue. According to Franz Tost, that is the master plan: "The media are better served than anywhere else. Not only do they experience the unveiling of the car, they are also able to experience the start of testing. They can take highly relevant pictures of the circuit – all in one go."

Everything seems to have been thought through – including the question of how one can make a silk cloth disappear into a refuelling nozzle. Yet even the best organisations should be allowed to keep a few secrets…

GP Australia

Results

1. David Coulthard
2. **Juan Pablo Montoya**
3. Kimi Räikkönen
4. Michael Schumacher
5. Jarno Trulli
6. Heinz-Harald Frentzen
7. Fernando Alonso
8. **Ralf Schumacher**

Pre-start: After the warm-up lap, Kimi Räikkönen heads immediately to the pits. Believing that the damp track surface will dry quickly, he changes from wet to dry tyres. At the front of the grid, Michael Schumacher, Rubens Barrichello, Heinz-Harald Frentzen and David Coulthard have decided to use wet tyres, whilst Juan Pablo Montoya and his team mate Ralf Schumacher have chosen dry tyres.

Start: Barrichello, starting alongside his team mate Michael Schumacher in the front row, suffers a false start. However, even this is not sufficient to take the lead from Michael Schumacher.

Lap 1: Michael Schumacher has a 1.5-second lead ahead of his team mate, whilst Nick Heidfeld battles his way up to third place.

Lap 2: Montoya manages to overtake Heidfeld. Race leader Michael Schumacher is already ten seconds ahead of the Colombian.

Lap 3: Coulthard makes a 7.2-second pit stop to change to dry tyres.

Lap 4: Montoya completes the quickest lap, ultimately showing that the time is now right for dry tyres.

Lap 6: In second place, Barrichello dramatically leaves the track at turn five.

Lap 7: Newcomer Ralph Firman has an accident at the same place. Michael Schumacher makes a pit stop for a tyre change.

Lap 9: Debris on the track forces the safety car into action. The line-up is now: Montoya ahead of Fernando Alonso, Jarno Trulli, Mark Webber and Olivier Panis.

Lap 11: Alonso takes advantage of the safety car phase to change tyres.

Lap 12: The race gets underway once again.

Lap 15: Montoya is able to extend his lead over Trulli to 6.9 seconds.

Lap 16: Webber leaves his defective Jaguar at the side of the track.

Lap 17: Both BMW WilliamsF1 Team drivers return to the pits. Montoya's pit stop lasts 9.2 seconds, but a wheel nut

jams during team mate Ralf Schumacher's pit stop, which takes 18.2 seconds. Back on the track, Ralf Schumacher spins at the first corner. Räikkönen takes the lead.

Lap 19: Webber's Jaguar is still on the track, and the safety car again takes over the race.

Lap 21: The race gets underway again, Räikkönen leads ahead of Michael Schumacher, Montoya is in sixth place, Ralf Schumacher in 14th place.

Lap 25: A misunderstanding brings both BAR drivers into the pits at the same time. Jenson Button has to wait until his team mate Jacques Villeneuve is ready.

Lap 38: After their pit stop, Räikkönen and Michael Schumacher are both battling it out behind Montoya for second place. The Ferrari driver launches an attack against Räikkönen in the first chicane. The Finn maintains his course, forcing the German onto the grass, and defends his position.

Lap 40: Räikkönen receives a drive-through penalty for exceeding the speed limit when approaching the pits. He drops down into seventh position.

Lap 43: Michael Schumacher briefly leaves the track, damaging both the air deflectors on his Ferrari, which fall off in succession.

Lap 46: The race marshals use the black and orange flag to request the Ferrari driver to return to the pits in order to completely remove all loose parts. After his pit stop, Michael Schumacher is in fourth place, and Montoya now leads ahead of Coulthard and Räikkönen.

Lap 48: Montoya spins, Coulthard takes the lead.

Lap 58: The Scot wins the race ahead of Montoya, Räikkönen and Michael Schumacher. Behind Trulli and Frentzen, in fifth and sixth place respectively, Alonso and Ralf Schumacher are the first drivers to benefit from points now being awarded to drivers finishing in seventh and eighth place.

Revolution from above

FIA president Max Mosley sees Formula One in danger – and sets in motion the most extensive changes to the regulations in the history of Formula One.

New teams, new drivers, new technology – it's all part of the new season. Yet what was being showcased at the 2003 inaugural race in Melbourne was the greatest change to the regulations in the history of Formula One. The points system, the qualification rounds, team orders, test drives and tyres – no stone has been left unturned.

Seeing danger for Formula One, FIA president Max Mosley has taken drastic measures: "Last season we lost two teams, namely Arrows and Prost. If we do nothing, we will lose a few more."

Mosley's basic objective for 2003 is to reign in the explosion in costs while increasing the opportunities for smaller teams.

It sounds good, yet it requires an extensive revision of the existing regulations. Within this context, the new points system sounds relatively simple. The previous system awarded points to the six best drivers (10-6-4-3-2-1 points). The new system awards points to the first eight drivers (10-8-6-5-4-3-2-1 points). This is set to enable smaller teams to win points on their own merit.

There has also been a minor adaptation of the regulation governing the use of replacement cars. Only in the case of a qualifying accident, a crash at the start of the race or an irreparable defect may teams use the "T-car".

The pit lane communications radio is still permitted, but everyone must be able to listen in. This applies to television spectators as well as to FIA bigwigs. The latter is included because with effect from this season, the order of finish can no longer be determined via team orders.

Drivers' electronic aids such as electronic traction control, automatic choke control or completely automatic transmission systems were originally meant to be banned with effect from the British Grand Prix on 20 July. Following fervent protests from some teams, however, the regulation has been revoked. This regulation was introduced at such short notice that most teams had already invested in this technology for the coming season. A ban for 2003 would bring about a lot of changes, but it would not reduce costs.

Where tyres are concerned, drastic measures have been taken. Tyre manufacturers Bridgestone and Michelin may now produce special combinations of tyre for each team, from which the team's managers can choose two types of dry tyre and one type of wet tyre for each Grand Prix.

A further amendment which will have a large impact concerns testing. Renault, Jaguar, Jordan and Minardi have accepted the proposal of the FIA and performed their test drives for two hours on the Friday morning of the race weekend. Consequently, between 1 March and 1 October, these teams are only allowed ten testing days outside of the Grand Prix weekends.

The newly created qualification sessions rules are equally revolutionary. On Fridays and Saturdays, two 75-minute qualification rounds take place. For each driver there is only one lap for individual qualifying times. The line-up for the Friday qualifying session follows the order of the World Championship table. On Saturday, the results of Friday's qualifying session are reversed to determine the day's line-up – suddenly in Formula One, the last shall be first. Yet that is not all: After the qualifying session on Saturday, all the cars are impounded in a "parc fermé" where only restricted types of work can take place – repairs, cleaning, checking the tyre pressure, changing the grease and lubricant. One thing is however not allowed: Changing the tyres and refuelling. This means that regardless of the racing tactic that the team considers to be right, thought must be given as to the fuel level before the final qualifying session. Those drivers who only want to make one refuelling stop during the race must accordingly take on board a lot of fuel. This can furthermore mean that a good starting position is sacrificed during qualifying. The reverse also applies: Drivers wishing to start at the front must carry as little weight as possible during final qualifying. Less weight means less fuel, but it also means an early first refuelling stop during the race. Regardless of how much fuel is being carried, no mistake may be made in the one decisive lap. If a driver makes a blunder or comes off the circuit, they may start from the back of the grid.

Saturday's "parc fermé", which serves as an interim storage site for the cars until the race itself, has one indisputable advantage – even the slightest suspicion that some form of hidden qualification session equipment is being used is dispelled.

The only technology onboard for final qualifying on Saturday is that which can withstand the race distance on Sunday. This ultimately spells an end to awfully expensive qualification engines, extra-light and thin disc brakes, mini-cooling systems and light clutches.

Discussion rages about the new regulations. Yet by the time the first race of the season in Melbourne had rolled around, the attitude of the BMW WilliamsF1 Team driver Juan Pablo Montoya was surely the correct one: "I'll take it as it comes."

Result

1. Kimi Räikkönen
2. Rubens Barrichello
3. Fernando Alonso
4. **Ralf Schumacher**
5. Jarno Trulli
6. Michael Schumacher
7. Jenson Button
8. Heinz-Harald Frentzen

GP Malaysia

Pre-start: Cristiano da Matta switches to using his replacement car and must therefore start from the pit lane. BAR-Honda driver Jacques Villeneuve fails to make it to the preliminary lap. For him, the race is over before it has even begun.

Start: Fernando Alonso, the youngest person ever to take pole position in the history of Formula One, immediately takes the lead. David Coulthard, who makes an impressive start, takes his place behind Alonso. In the second bend, Michael Schumacher's attempts to force Coulthard out of second place result in him colliding with Jarno Trulli's tail, thus causing Trulli to spin. In the confusion, Antonio Pizzonia hits Juan Pablo Montoya's tail. Flying debris tears away Jos Verstappen's tail wing. Pizzonia, Verstappen and Montoya are forced into the pits. The Colombian will no longer play a role in this race. Three laps behind, he will finish a distant twelfth place.

Lap 1: Alonso leads ahead of Coulthard, Nick Heidfeld, Kimi Räikkönen, Jenson Button, Rubens Barrichello and Olivier Panis. Ralf Schumacher is in ninth position, his brother in twelfth.

Lap 3: Coulthard is forced out of the race by problems with

the electronics. Alonso now leads ahead of Räikkönen, who has overtaken Heidfeld.

Lap 4: Michael Schumacher comes into the pits to have a new front wing fitted. He also uses the stop to refuel. He re-enters the race in 14th place.

Lap 10: The race marshals believe that Michael Schumacher's collision with Trulli was avoidable. As a penalty, the Ferrari driver must therefore drive slowly through the pit lane. Barrichello pushes Heidfeld out of third place.

Lap 12: Panis – in fifth place – comes in for a pit stop. Half a lap later, he is forced to quit the race because of steam bubbles in the fuel system.

Lap 13: Heidfeld's engine stalls whilst in the pits. After 23.1 seconds stopped in the pits he is only in eleventh position.

Lap 15: Alonso enters the pits; Räikkönen is now leading ahead of Barrichello.

Lap 22: After completing the first refuelling phase, Räikkönen leads ahead of Alonso, Barrichello, Ralf Schumacher, Button and Trulli.

Lap 35: Trulli makes his second pit stop; Räikkönen now leads by more than 20 seconds ahead of Barrichello.

Lap 41: After Barrichello, Räikkönen also completes his pit stop. The Finn is able to retain his lead ahead of Barrichello; Alonso is third. Ralf Schumacher comes into the pits and holds on to fourth place. His brother, Michael, passes Trulli and Button and eases his way into fifth place.

Lap 44: When he comes in for refuelling, Michael Schumacher loses both places again to Button and Trulli.

Lap 51: Trulli's car spins when taking on Button, but he is still able to keep Michael Schumacher from taking sixth place.

Lap 56: Räikkönen celebrates the first Grand Prix victory of his career. He is joined on the podium by Barrichello and Alonso. Ralf Schumacher, in fourth place, is the last driver who was not lapped. Immediately before the end of the race, Trulli and Michael Schumacher even manage to overtake Button, who now finishes in seventh place ahead of Heinz-Harald Frentzen.

The first time

Just how good am I? This is the question asked by everyone in motor sport. The first Formula One victory is a comforting reply.

What does a true racing driver decide to do when he takes third place on the winners' podium? He decides that next time, he wants be two places further up. During the victory celebrations in Melbourne, you could see from Kimi Räikkönen's face that this very thought was running through his head. At the Australian Grand Prix, his failed pit stop stood in the way of his victory, yet two weeks later in Kuala Lumpur the time had come – Kimi Räikkönen won his first Formula One race. It was his 35th Formula One race and his 58th race overall. At 23 years old, Räikkönen is the third-youngest Grand Prix winner. Only Jacky Ickx was younger, and a certain Bruce McLaren, who provided the name for the team where Räikkönen is now enjoying success.

The first Formula One victory! McLaren boss Ron Dennis immediately puts this victory into the perspective of a long-serving team owner: "The first victory is like a noose around the neck of each driver. The sooner you pull your head out of it, the sooner you can continue to develop as a driver." Such philosophical words are mostly met with youthful scepticism from up-and-coming racing drivers at the outset of their career. Whoever enters the world of Formula One, the recognised pinnacle of international motor sport, automatically belongs to the elite of racing drivers. He is on the stony path to the top, where success and victory abound. At what point and why should a Formula One victory be a problem for such sportsmen?

Nobody has managed to explain this as openly and honestly as Räikkönen's fellow countryman, his friend and supporter Mika Häkkinen. The two-times World Champion, who, driving an inferior Lotus 102B-Judd, took winner's points with his fifth-place finish in only his third race, considered this achievement to be completely normal. "At the time, I was totally convinced that it would only be a question of several races until I took my place at the top of the podium, and from then on I would fight for the World Championship title." The reason for Häkkinen's optimism: "I was used to this way of thinking from the other racing classes, and was unable to imagine things any differently in Formula One." However, the reality for Häkkinen was quite different. It took the blonde Finn 96 races to be the first to see the black and white chequered flag. It is a moment that makes even grown men cry. Let's not forget Jean Alesi, who after 91 Grand Prix races was so moved by the greatness of the moment at the 1995 race in Montreal that "during the last laps of the race, I was unable to make out the track for the tears in my eyes".

The first ever Formula One victory is truly something special. For the three-times World Champion Jackie Stewart, the initial Grand Prix victory is the greatest triumph of all: "Suddenly, a Formula One driver becomes a Grand Prix winner. At least on this occasion, you are among the world's finest. That cannot be taken away."

It is something which transcends time. In a sport with continuous new successes and defeats, it is something which endures. Michael Schumacher, who began his list of 70 victories at Spa in 1992, said: "It's a milestone in my career that nobody can take away from me."

The three-times World Champion Niki Lauda views it with slightly less emotion, but still gives it the same importance: "The first victory provides calm within the team. You have proven to everybody that you are capable of doing it. Now it is the team's duty to continue to provide the driver with the technology that will enable further victories to be won." Following his first-place victory, this very perception strikes a chord with the otherwise taciturn Kimi, and he coolly says: "At least nobody else will be asking me when I'm going to win my first race." And, as a postscript, just to gain a small insight into the inner life of a racing driver: "Even if I never win another race in my career, this day will remain with me for ever."

GP Brazil

Results

1. Giancarlo Fisichella
2. Kimi Räikkönen
3. Fernando Alonso
4. David Coulthard
5. Heinz-Harald Frentzen
6. Jacques Villeneuve
7. **Ralf Schumacher**
8. Jarno Trulli

Pre-Start: Because of heavy rain, the race marshals decide to postpone the start of the race by 15 minutes and to begin the race with a safety car phase.

Start: Safety car driver Bernd Mayländer leads the field into the first lap.

Lap 1: Olivier Panis makes a refuelling stop.

Lap 8: Giancarlo Fisichella also makes a refuelling stop.

Lap 9: The safety car opens up the race. David Coulthard out-accelerates Rubens Barrichello and places himself in the lead; Kimi Räikkönen pushes Mark Webber from third place.

Lap 10: Räikkönen moves past Barrichello. Juan Pablo Montoya, already ahead of Webber, is also able to overtake the Brazilian. Ralf Schumacher is in sixth position.

Lap 11: Räikkönen takes the lead from Coulthard, with Montoya also overtaking the Scot. Ralf Schumacher's car goes into a spin – eleventh position.

Lap 15: Coulthard claws back second place from Montoya.

Lap 16: Michael Schumacher overtakes Montoya and is now in third place.

Lap 18: Whilst on the finishing straight, the front right wheel suspension collapses on Ralph Firman's Jordan. Firman spins out of the race and in doing so hits the tail of Panis' Toyota. Numerous pieces of debris across the track cause the safety car to be deployed. Most drivers use the safety car phase to refuel.

Lap 23: The all-clear is given to resume the race; a spin forces Heinz-Harald Frentzen from eighth into last position.

Lap 24: Montoya overtakes Cristiano da Matta, but moments later skids and leaves the track at turn three. Directly behind him, Antonio Pizzonia goes into a spin and hits Montoya's WilliamsF1 BMW FW25.

Lap 27: At turn three Michael Schumacher suffers the same fate as Montoya and Pizzonia before him – his car aquaplanes and slides off the racetrack. For the third time, the safety car is called into action. Räikkönen and da Matta refuel. The line-up behind the safety car: Coulthard ahead of Barrichello, Ralf Schumacher, Webber, Jenson Button, Fernando Alonso.

Lap 30: The all-clear is given for the race to resume.

Lap 33: After Jos Verstappen, Button and Jacques Ville-

neuve all leave the track at turn three, the safety car once again takes control of the race.

Lap 37: Restart – Coulthard leads ahead of Barrichello, Ralf Schumacher, Alonso, Räikkönen and Fisichella.

Lap 38: Räikkönen overtakes Alonso and Ralf Schumacher – fourth position.

Lap 42: For overtaking whilst the yellow flag was out, Alonso must complete a drive-through penalty in the pit lane, which sees him drop from fourth position to ninth.

Lap 45: Barrichello is successful in overtaking Coulthard at the end of the finishing straight – the Brazilian immediately breaks away.

Lap 47: Leading by more than four seconds, injection nozzle trouble forces Barrichello out of the race.

Lap 48: In fourth position, Ralf Schumacher enters the pits to refuel. He re-enters the race in ninth position.

Lap 52: Race leader Coulthard makes a refuelling stop and rejoins the race in fourth place.

Lap 54: At this stage of the race the Bridgestone tyres are superior to the Michelin tyres. Jordan driver Fisichella is therefore able to overtake Räikkönen, whose car is fitted with Michelin tyres, and he immediately increases the distance between them. In the meantime, Webber has an accident in the home bend whilst travelling at 300 km/h. With debris strewn across the track, the safety car is deployed.

Lap 55: Despite clear flag signals, Alonso hits the wreckage at full speed.

Lap 56: Fisichella passes the wreckage slowly and crosses the finishing line. Räikkönen uses the safety car phase to refuel. The race is red-flagged and brought to an early end on lap 55. If the race is stopped when over 75% complete, the results are declared using the positions two laps prior to the red flag being shown. Fisichella celebrates, but Räikkönen is named as the winner. Three days later, the FIA realises that Fisichella had already started his 56th lap at the time when the race was stopped, thus meaning that the 54th lap is used to determine the race results. Fisichella is subsequently named as the winner and Webber, originally in seventh place, no longer qualifies for points. By contrast, Ralf Schumacher improves from ninth to seventh place.

Happiness after the hard work

In desperate times, a wet weather race can sometimes mean salvation.

The occasion: The 200th Grand Prix of the Jordan Team. A small and refined celebration, which only eleven Formula One racing teams have achieved to this day. At such events, many congratulatory words are spoken, and many flattering statements are made. Yet if on this cloudy Sunday in the bustling Brazilian city of São Paulo somebody had said to Eddie Jordan, the team's maverick boss, that it would become his day of victory, then even the Irishman, renowned for his professional optimism, would have smiled.

Since the inception of the Jordan Grand Prix Team in 1991, the promises of anticipated success made by the team's boss have been true works of art – it was just a question of waiting a little while for the victories to mount up. Yet the season did not begin in this way. The "enfant terrible" of Formula One had become unusually quiet. Nobody in the team spoke of victories, not even Eddie Jordan. He let it be known that it would be sufficient for him if his team simply survived the year.

The lover of chic spectacles with a good eye for a quick deal had suffered several blows in previous months. At the end of 2002, he lost his main sponsor, Deutsche Post, as well as its subsidiary DHL. His engine partners, Honda, also terminated their cooperation agreement with Jordan in order to devote more resources to their joint effort with the BAR Team. Jordan had to react. Around 100 employees were made redundant. In the drivers' area, rumours were flying that the annual budget had been slashed from € 155m to approximately € 60m. There was also talk that the Ford Cosworth engines, worth around € 18m,

would have to be paid for. Up until that point, the team had received free engines from Honda. The usually optimistic Eddie Jordan specified his difficulty: "The sponsoring market has shrunk by approximately 30% in comparison to the previous year. For teams such as mine, it is a question of survival."

Yet in the drivers' area, only one thing matters: If there ever was somebody able to avoid a crisis, it is Eddie Jordan. His entry into Formula One, surviving the initial years, the art of juggling all responsibilities in the air – it was both a job and a calling for the trained bank clerk. For this reason, everybody was excited when in 1999 the team seemed to have broken through into the top ranks of Formula One racing. Two victories in one season and a Jordan driver who was almost in the running for the World Championship title until the very end of the season. After this year, everything seemed possible. Yet instead of ranking amongst the top teams, confusion followed as Eddie Jordan himself admits: "After the success, huge amounts of money were available. I wanted to use the opportunity and I invested like mad and employed many people. Suddenly we had gone from having a workforce of 200 to 300 employees."

Size does not necessarily mean more success, as Jordan had to learn. "The company grew too quickly. Before we were a manageable and collegiate team. Yet suddenly, a great number of younger engineers and managers entered that team, and our experienced employees no longer felt happy there and left. We lost our corporate culture. It was a disaster."

It is a disaster, however, from which lessons have been learned. The team was scaled down and Jordan introduced a strict cost management system: "Irrespective of the department – logistics, technology or anywhere else – every employee had to make a weekly note of where costs had been saved. Everyone. Instead of six or seven cars a season, we now only build three. We no longer order components without first checking. We don't let the warehouse overflow any more."

Despite this, nobody has become rich from making savings alone. Anyone who sees this year's Jordan-Cosworth EJ13 will see a suspiciously large amount of yellow bodywork free of sponsors' names. Jordan, a team for which all active German Formula One drivers apart from Nick Heidfeld have driven at some point in their career, needs – in Jordan's own words: "The magician Houdini on top form – able to pull out lots of rabbits from his hat." Takeover offers, such as that from Red Bull boss Dietrich Mateschitz, have been turned down by Jordan, who attaches a great deal of importance to independence. Instead, the Irishman with a rock 'n roll image is hoping to continue as the "dark horse" of elite racing. Since 1998, Jordan has been the only team able to achieve Grand Prix victories alongside today's top teams, namely Ferrari, BMW WilliamsF1 Team and McLaren. There have been four victories overall, three of which took place in chaotic wet weather races. This is generally typical for Jordan: The fewer chances one has, the more important it is to use them...

A silent goodbye

A lot spoke in favour of carrying on. Yet the one thing that the position of BMW Motorsport Director could not offer Gerhard Berger was boredom.

No, Gerhard Berger is not a late riser. "Waking up between seven and eight in the morning would be ideal." So, let's base the following on this ideal scenario. It is 7.30 in the morning, and Gerhard Berger is waking up in his Monaco home. Slowly, the first thoughts of the day take root. Yes, the garage has already been cleared up. He has played and run around with his two younger daughters, Heidi and Sarah, yesterday, the day before yesterday and even the day before that – they will be happy to be left alone for once. No memorandum has to be written and distributed to the Board today. Furthermore, the BMW WilliamsF1 Team has been winning for a long time without his help. Only the dog, Lucky, wants to go walkies – but that can wait an hour or two. In Gerhard Berger's head, all his thoughts come together to form a completely new realisation – he has no plans, no duties, no targets. Instead, he is left with a tremendous feeling of not knowing what he should do today. Boredom! Gerhard Berger closes his eyes and smiles happily.

It may sound like a paradox, but when Gerhard Berger is asked today what caused him to withdraw into his private life after five years as BMW Motorsport Director, he cites his desire for boredom: "In recent years, my life was so hectic that even on holiday, I always decided in advance how to structure the day. What I have to do, when I will sit down, when I will make some notes, when I can take care of this or that. I simply could not manage to go without planning the day. I'm thoroughly sick of it. I long for a couple of days of boredom."

The Tyrolean with a flair for making the right decisions now found himself faced with a difficult choice. He hesitated for a long time before giving up his position at BMW. Both the lure of the job and his congenial colleagues weighed in heavily on the side of staying.

"A mighty tug-of-war was going on in my head. There were days when things were perfectly clear. And then there were days when I gave serious thought to carrying on. Working for BMW is great; there are people there who are fantastic to work with."

The first of such people Berger mentions is the man whose appointment aroused some scepticism: BMW Motorsport Director Dr Mario Theissen. A double act in the BMW Motorsport management! The ex-Formula One star, Gerhard Berger, with an inclination for the exotic, and engine specialist Dr Mario Theissen, a BMW technician through and through, but without a great deal of Formula One experience. Today, Berger now knows one thing: "No matter where I work or in which position, it will be difficult to find a partner like Mario. We complement each other well, work well together and have an open working relationship."

This double act worked so well that at the end of his period of service, Gerhard Berger can look back on a series of accomplishments: "Within the context of what my original undertaking was and what I am now leaving behind after five years of service, I believe that the task has been perfectly completed for BMW. They were five successful years of motor sport, starting with the Le Mans victory in 1999 and extending up to last year's runner-up position in the For-

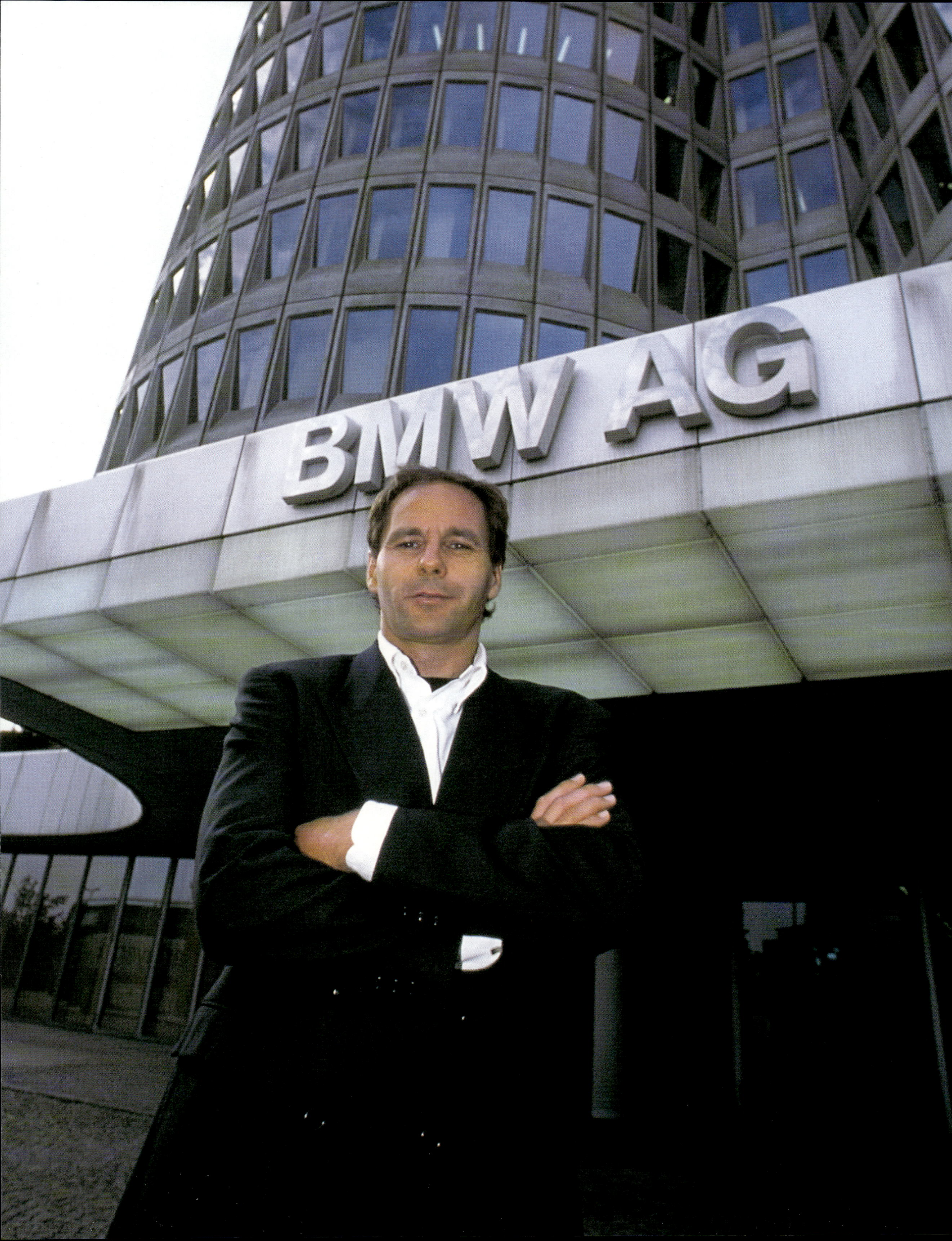
BMW AG

mula One Constructors' World Championship. The Touring Car events and Formula BMW have also evolved rapidly within the same period of time. We have moved forward on all fronts and really endeavoured to position BMW everywhere in a way befitting of BMW – not just with regard to sport, but also its image."

Berger has given a lot to BMW, and BMW has given a lot to Berger. The good-humoured Tyrolean has remained true to himself, and yet he has changed. This can be described by his colleague, Dr Mario Theissen: "As a person, he has remained completely unchanged. So, too, has he in his role as a specialist and expert. There has been some change, however, as he has gained an insight into the workings of a large company, as well as an insight into project management and the structuring of a large team. He will certainly take that experience with him. Furthermore, over the course of the years he has developed an understanding of how to work effectively in such an environment."

These were, and continue to be the demands, demands which even someone such as Gerhard Berger had some difficulty in meeting at the outset – something he openly admits to: "As a racing driver, you have to be somewhat of an egoist. Ultimately the racing driver is the last link in the chain, the person responsible for putting all the plans into action on a Sunday afternoon, alone in the racing car against the others. You have to battle through against everyone and anyone who comes between you and your objective. If you are working in a group further up the chain, however, then the focus is on teamwork. Under such circumstances one has to change, and that isn't at all simple."

Simple it may not be, but it is very satisfying indeed: "Yes, we have put in many years of hard work and seen to it that we have brought to BMW the right people with the right philosophy. I think in that we have been successful." The people in the team went together as well as the various pieces of technical equipment, and still do. Berger, who in his 14 years as a Formula One racing driver spent nine seasons racing for the elite McLaren and Ferrari teams, was able to assess what BMW in Munich had to offer straight away: "I immediately understood what goes on in the FIZ (Research and Innovation Centre). It was instantly clear to me that if we were in a position to use these resources for ourselves, the others would look outdated. I can still remember that when I first started I was ridiculed by the competition. Time and time again they said: 'Gerhard, you must be mad. You want to get involved with the Group's motor sport arm and even build Formula One engines? In that case, you will have to get an engine builder with a great deal of Formula One experience.' I was ridiculed. But from the first day I was certain: We must make full use of technology to establish ourselves in motor sport. Furthermore, it must be ensured that the motor sport unit is working according to the rules of motor sport, as well as taking advantage of the Group's resources and systems. They are much further advanced than the other engine builders out there. We have completely different processes and completely different opportunities. I believe that we at BMW have successfully combined the sport and the Group."

The successes of these five years are amazing, starting with the on-schedule production of the first Formula One E41

Inside BMW

37

engine, its launch at Melbourne in 2000 and finish in the top three in its inaugural race. The first victory in Imola in 2001, first ever pole position at Magny-Cours in 2001, runner-up in the World Championship title in 2002 and the fight for the title in 2003. Yet when asked about what he considers to be the highlight of his tenure, Berger goes right back to the beginning: "For me, it was winning the Le Mans 24-hour race. One person was boasting that he could change his gearbox in five minutes, another was boasting that he would win, and another said he had such a huge budget that no other person stood a chance. We had neither the budget, nor were we able to change the gearbox in five minutes. In fact, we didn't build a long distance car at all. What we built was a go-kart that would last for precisely 24 hours and then we put the quickest drivers in it. This is how we got through the race and how we won the race. The race and the victory were a wonderful experience for me."

This vehicle, the BMW V12 LMR, is also the car he would wish for if he were to ask for something from BMW after his retirement: "If I am completely honest, I have given much thought to the question of whether it would not be nice, at the end of my five years with BMW, to drive all those cars which were crucial to BMW's success over those five years."

That could be a plan for the near future. He is also planning on becoming more involved in his parents' forwarding company in the coming months. "At the moment I am dedicating more and more time to it because it is an extremely difficult time for the industry. But it is not my livelihood, nor is it what I want to do in the future, nor is it something that I am passionate about. There are many emotions involved because it is my parents' business and because I grew up with a lot of these people."

His passion, on the other hand, lies in motor sport. For this reason, Gerhard Berger must discover how, and if, he can live without it: "It's hard to say. First of all I want to find out whether I miss being an active player in motor sport. If I don't miss it, I would have no problem in giving it up. If I do miss it, I'll take a look around and find myself a new challenge in the sport."

And if it is not motor sport, there are plenty of alternatives: "I have investments in a wide range of areas – companies, properties and businesses – which interest me. I have thousands of ideas as to what I could do," says Gerhard Berger, laughing at himself. "I think I am the wrong type of person to get really bored…"

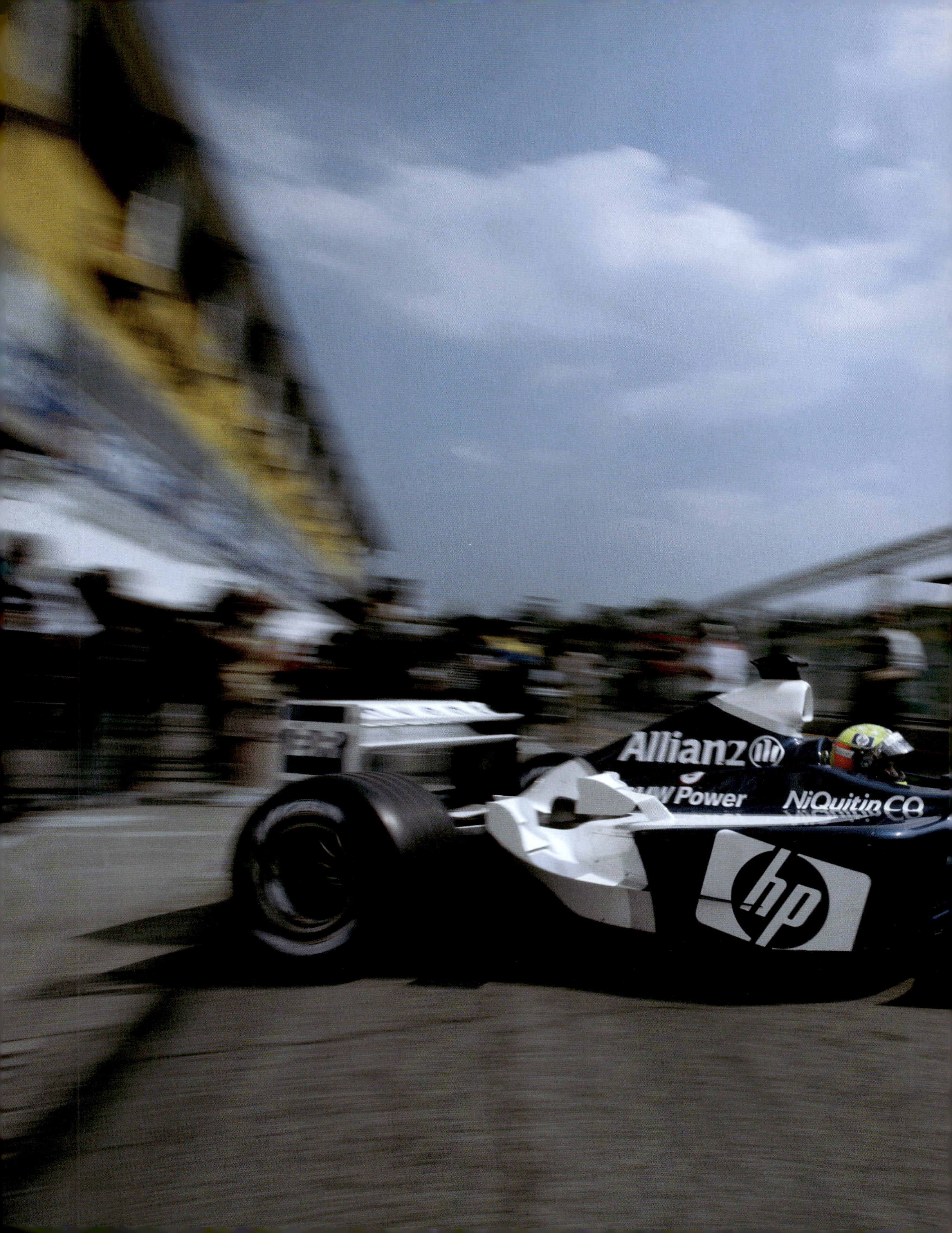
Allianz
NiQuitin CQ
hp

GP San Marino

Results

1. Michael Schumacher
2. Kimi Räikkönen
3. Rubens Barrichello
4. **Ralf Schumacher**
5. David Coulthard
6. Fernando Alonso
7. **Juan Pablo Montoya**
8. Jenson Button

Start: Ralf Schumacher gets off to the best start, retaining his lead ahead of his brother as they enter the first chicane. Behind the two brothers, Rubens Barrichello is put under pressure from Juan Pablo Montoya and Kimi Räikkönen. The biggest loser at the start of the race is Jaguar's Mark Webber, who is unable to take advantage of his outstanding fifth place on the grid and immediately loses six places. Worse still, Jos Verstappen, Ralph Firman and Justin Wilson must all start from the pit lane.

Lap 3: Ralf and Michael Schumacher fight it out for first place.
Lap 4: The two brothers cross the start/finish line neck and neck, yet Ralf Schumacher maintains his lead.
Lap 8: The line-up at the front of the race has stabilised: Ralf Schumacher leads ahead of his brother Michael, followed by Barrichello, Montoya, Räikkönen and Fernando Alonso.
Lap 15: During his refuelling stop, Webber fails to observe the maximum speed limit for the pit lane and receives a drive-through penalty.
Lap 16: Ralf Schumacher, clearly driving with a three-stop strategy, comes in for his first pit stop.
Lap 17: Michael Schumacher, who up until now has tried in vain to overtake his brother, immediately makes the most of the clear track ahead of him to clock a quick lap time. Following their pit stops, Barrichello and Montoya are in fifth and sixth position respectively.
Lap 18: Michael Schumacher comes into the pits, enabling the McLaren drivers, both with a two-stop strategy, to take the lead. Michael Schumacher's pit stop is short enough for him to re-enter the race in third position ahead of his brother.
Lap 22: After his team mate David Coulthard, race leader Räikkönen now makes his refuelling stop. Michael Schumacher is now in the lead, whilst behind him Ralf Schumacher is put under pressure from Barrichello.
Lap 30: Montoya wants to make his second refuelling stop, but there is a problem with the refuelling unit. Without having achieved anything he returns to the race. Two laps later he successfully completes his pit stop.
Lap 31: Ralf Schumacher drops from second to fourth place following his pit stop.
Lap 34: After making his refuelling stop, Michael Schumacher re-enters the track ahead of Räikkönen. Both drivers have still to make one more pit stop each.
Lap 44: Räikkönen's pit stop allows Barrichello and Ralf Schumacher to overtake him. However, unlike the other two drivers, Räikkönen does not have to make a third pit stop.
Lap 45: A moment of panic at Ferrari: For a fraction of a second, race leader Michael Schumacher loses his concentration and briefly comes off the track in the Rivazza bend. Despite this, the Ferrari driver still leads the race.
Lap 48: Ralf Schumacher makes his third pit stop. He drops down to fourth place behind Barrichello and Räikkönen.
Lap 49: Barrichello takes the lead for one lap because his team mate is making his final pit stop.
Lap 50: Barrichello's pit stop does not go as smoothly. A wheel nut jams – the Brazilian drops down to fourth place behind Ralf Schumacher.
Lap 53: Following a duel, Barrichello pushes ahead of Ralf Schumacher to take third place.
Lap 61: Michael Schumacher comes in for his 65th Grand Prix victory ahead of the championship leader Räikkönen.

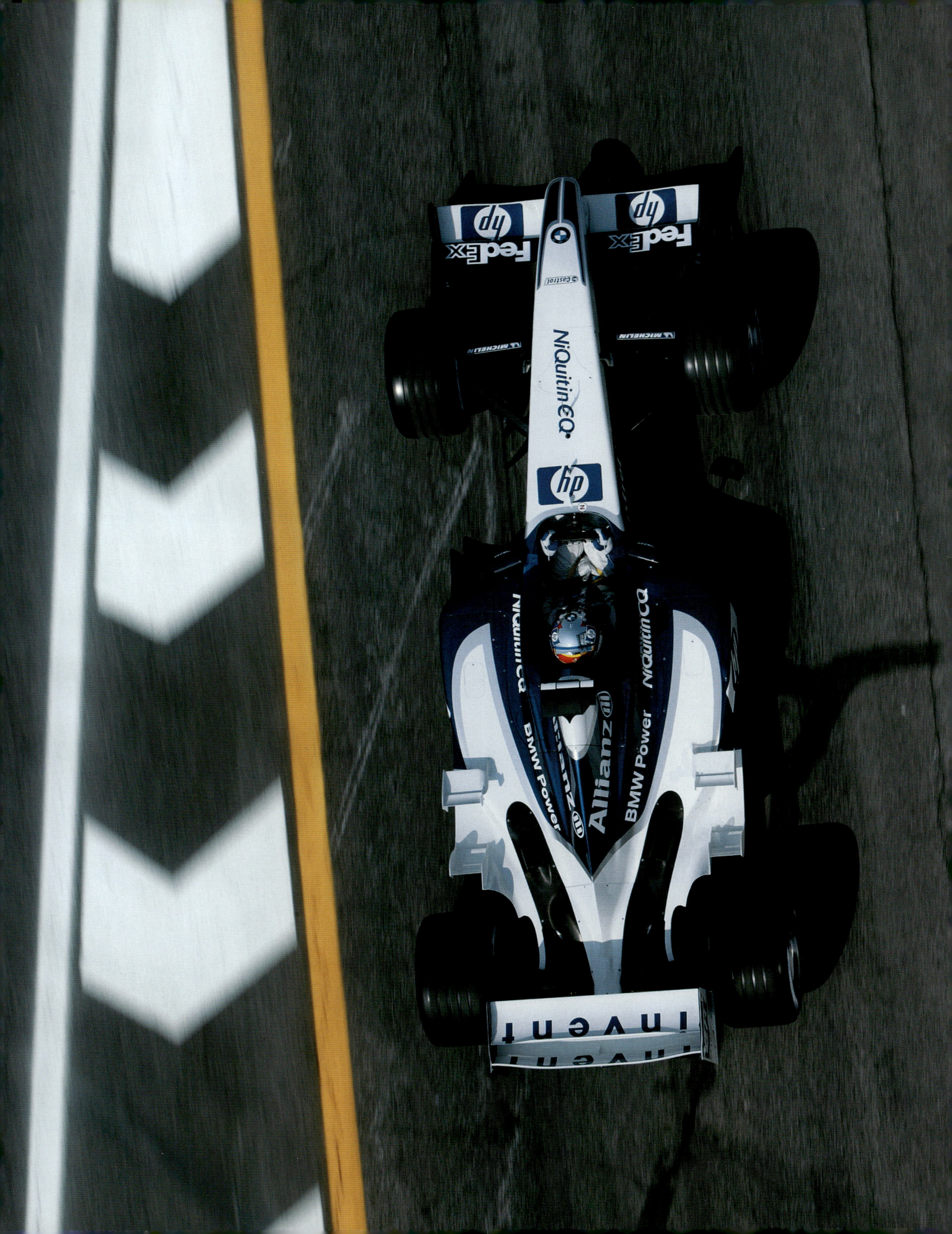

hp
FedEx
NiQuitin CQ
Allianz
BMW Power
invent

The last victory of the Red Goddess

Many people had already written off Ferrari and Michael Schumacher. Reason enough for the "Reds" to show everyone the very opposite.

It was a made-to-measure race for the Italians – the San Marino Grand Prix. This is exactly how the aficionados of Michael Schumacher and the Ferrari team expect things to be: Pole position, fastest lap time, victory. The situation at the first three races of the season had been the very opposite: Risk, records and victory had been replaced by failure, flops and floundering. Three races and at least as many mistakes – that was the criticism thrown at the Reds by the critics. And they had the proof to do so.

The Australian Grand Prix – the start of the season. An unlucky choice of tyres at the start of the race, followed by a bungled pit stop and then a rare mistake from the five-time World Champion as he briefly comes off the track on two occasions, thereby damaging his car.

The Malaysian Grand Prix – once again, the World Champion is in trouble. On the second bend he collides with Jarno Trulli. The fitting of a new front wing and a slow drive through the pit lane costs him a great deal of time. The Brazilian Grand Prix was a temporary low for Ferrari: Michael Schumacher's car aquaplanes and shoots off the track whilst Rubens Barrichello, leading the race, coasts to a standstill due to a lack of fuel.

After this opening, the Ferrari team had considerably fewer points than Renault, and their two drivers, Barrichello and Michael Schumacher, were in seventh and eighth positions respectively in the World Championship table – a far cry from their usual ranking.

Keeping one's cool in such a time of vulnerability and criticism is one of the main tasks faced by a leading Formula One team. Accordingly, Ferrari's Race Director, Jean Todt, did not miss an opportunity to commit everyone to his statement of faith: "At the moment, the most important thing for our team is not to fall into a state of panic, but instead to understand what allowed these mistakes to occur. None of these mistakes has called into question the actual chances of the team, its drivers, its tyres or its cars."

These words from Todt were just as supportive to the team as they were indicative of the approval of the F2002 which had been used in the initial races. Having accumulated 221 World Championship points, last season's F2002 became the most successful Ferrari in the 53-year-old history of the World Championship. It was not without reason that the media named this car the "Red Goddess".

However, the intention was finally to retire the car before the race in Imola. The aim was to showcase the successor model, the F2003-GA, for the first time this season in front of a home crowd. The race preparation reliability test comprises four complete race distances completed in the testing facility, but this could not be confirmed prior to the San Marino Grand Prix. Just as they would have liked to excite the fans with the new bearer of hope, two engine failures in the days prior to the race at Imola stood in the way of it being put into action.

After a problematic start to the season, hopes of properly initiating the battle for the title at the first race on European soil using the F2003-GA – considered to be an outstandingly fast car – were dashed. Once again, the team would have to put their faith in the Red Goddess.

It was a trust that was rewarded, and one which put the shaky start to the season into context. Unsettled weather and accidents alone made the first three World Championship races quite untypical – with regard to both the race itself and the final result.

These races could not be invoked for assessing the actual relative power among the elite racing teams. On the other hand, the Grand Prix in San Marino was the first "normal" race of the season where these aspects were concerned. It became the first race of the season in which one team and one driver achieved pole position, fastest lap time and victory. It is this very situation which allows BMW Motorsport Director, Gerhard Berger, to attribute both Ferrari's struggle at the start of the season and their first victory of 2003 to a common denominator: "The whole talk in the past few weeks was nonsense. Anyone who really thought or thinks that Michael Schumacher is not a serious competitor for this year's title hasn't the faintest idea about this business."

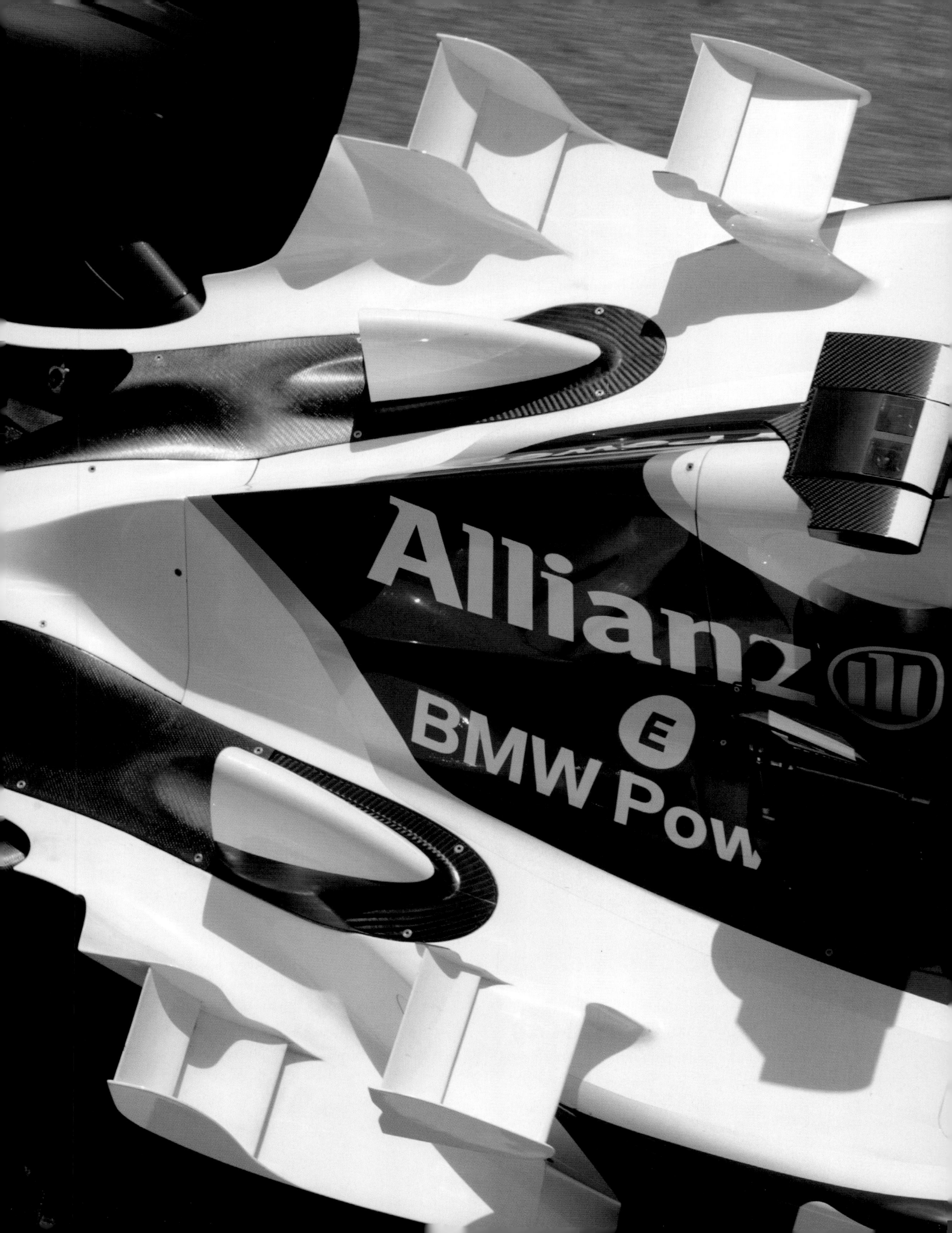
Allianz
BMW Pow

Results

1. Michael Schumacher
2. Fernando Alonso
3. Rubens Barrichello
4. **Juan Pablo Montoya**
5. **Ralf Schumacher**
6. Cristiano da Matta
7. Mark Webber
8. Ralph Firman

GP Spain

Start: For the World Championship leader, the race is over before he has even crossed the start line. Kimi Räikkönen, starting from the last row due to skidding off the circuit during training, careers into the tail of Antonio Pizzonia's Jaguar, whose automatic choke has failed. At the head of the race, Fernando Alonso gets off to an outstanding start. He manages to out-accelerate Rubens Barrichello, and almost edges ahead of Michael Schumacher. At the first corner, however, Barrichello is successful in getting ahead of Alonso. The Brazilian and his team mate Michael Schumacher almost collide. A real collision occurs in the battle for fourth place: Jarno Trulli touches the rear wheel of David Coulthard's McLaren. This causes the Scot to spin, but for Trulli the race is over. Due to the accident between Pizzonia and Räikkönen, the safety car is deployed. Heinz-Harald Frentzen, Ralph Firman and Coulthard take advantage of the safety car phase to make a pit stop.

Lap 6: The race gets underway again, and Juan Pablo Montoya locks his front tyres to out-brake Jenson Button in the fight for fifth place.

Lap 7: Michael Schumacher leads the race by 2.1 seconds ahead of Barrichello, who is coming under pressure from Alonso. Ralf Schumacher is in fourth place.

Lap 17: Alonso is the first of the leading drivers to make a refuelling stop.

Lap 18: Button and Coulthard collide in the first bend. Button requires a new BAR nose, whilst Coulthard is left stuck in the gravel.

Lap 19: Michael Schumacher enters the pits, thus placing Barrichello in the lead. Montoya, in third place, also makes a refuelling stop, causing him to drop behind Alonso and Ralf Schumacher.

Lap 35: Michael Schumacher refuels once again – in front of 96,000 spectators, local hero Alonso takes the lead.

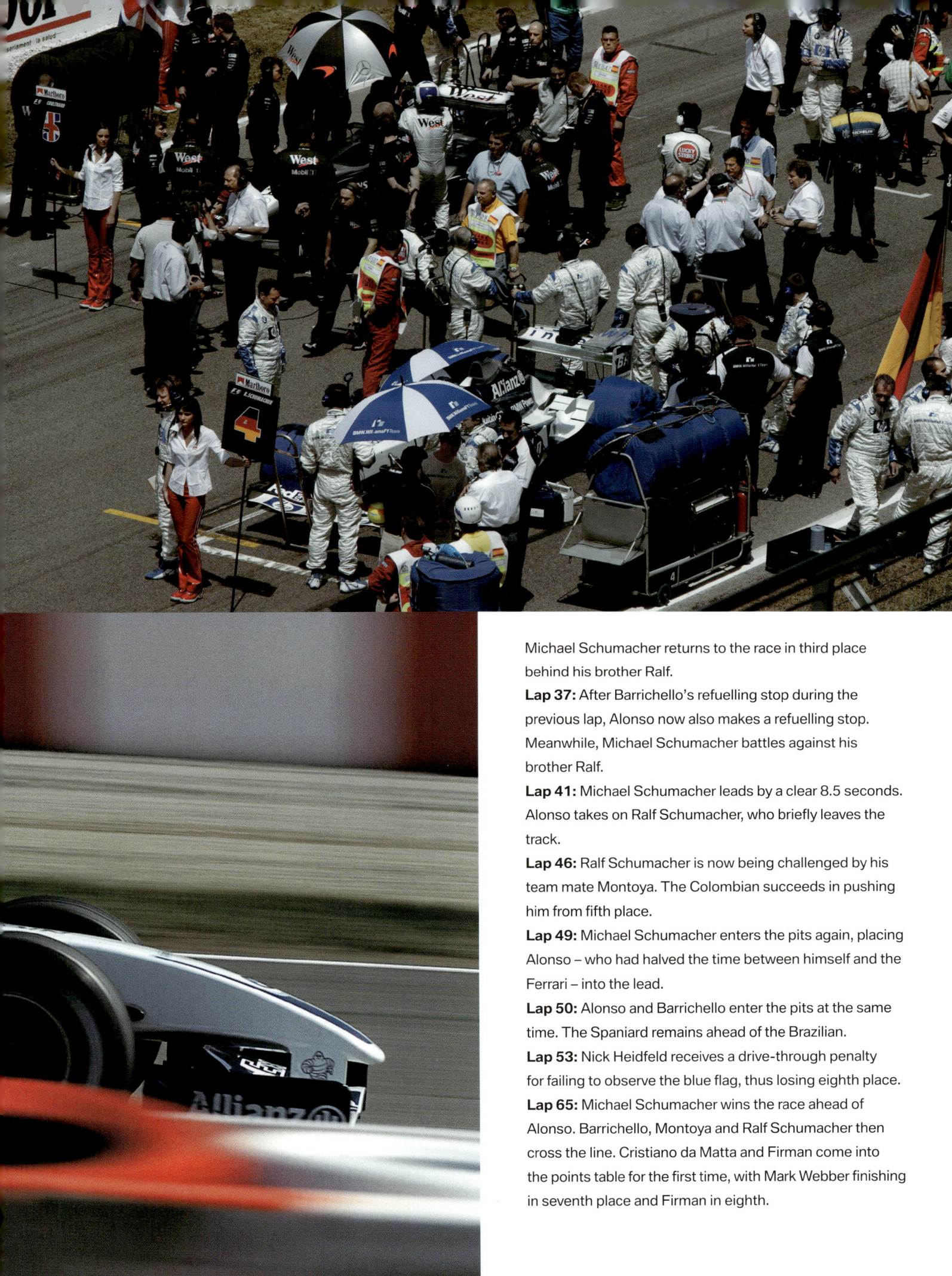

Michael Schumacher returns to the race in third place behind his brother Ralf.

Lap 37: After Barrichello's refuelling stop during the previous lap, Alonso now also makes a refuelling stop. Meanwhile, Michael Schumacher battles against his brother Ralf.

Lap 41: Michael Schumacher leads by a clear 8.5 seconds. Alonso takes on Ralf Schumacher, who briefly leaves the track.

Lap 46: Ralf Schumacher is now being challenged by his team mate Montoya. The Colombian succeeds in pushing him from fifth place.

Lap 49: Michael Schumacher enters the pits again, placing Alonso – who had halved the time between himself and the Ferrari – into the lead.

Lap 50: Alonso and Barrichello enter the pits at the same time. The Spaniard remains ahead of the Brazilian.

Lap 53: Nick Heidfeld receives a drive-through penalty for failing to observe the blue flag, thus losing eighth place.

Lap 65: Michael Schumacher wins the race ahead of Alonso. Barrichello, Montoya and Ralf Schumacher then cross the line. Cristiano da Matta and Firman come into the points table for the first time, with Mark Webber finishing in seventh place and Firman in eighth.

Lap by Lap **GP Spain**

At the height of fashion

Caps, T-shirts, jewel encrusted tops – the white and blue colours of BMW can arouse fascination at the track side too.

"Will the door open on time?" "Is the dry ice ready?" "Are the hostesses in their places?"
At 8.20 p.m. on the dot, everything is set: The dry ice is ready, the hostesses are in position. The doors open to 300 invited guests. The doors open for the presentation of the new BMW WilliamsF1 Team collection in Barcelona. The doors open for premium quality outfits for women, men and children, accompanied by numerous fashionable sporting accessories.

Regardless of whether it is the team line, the Juan Pablo Montoya line or the Ralf Schumacher line featuring shirts, pullovers, jackets and caps, one thing can always be noted with regard to BMW. According to Thomas Giuliani, the Director of Marketing Communication at BMW Group: "We have evolved, our collection has become more striking. Today there is more of a fashion element than there used to be, compared to when everything was primarily sport oriented." Fashion wants to be presented in a fashionable way. In accordance with this notion, the Barcelona event had been meticulously planned and organised since the beginning of January. It was assigned very clear targets, which Giuliani formulates as follows: "The event must be befitting of us. It must be modern and innovative, it should support our brand values, thus it should convey a mixture of dynamism and culture." Three locations were shortlisted for the event. However, none of them was so futuristic, so extravagant and yet at the same time so communications oriented as the "Torre de Telefónica", designed by leading Spanish architect Santiago Calatrava, who designed the 136 m-high construction, reminiscent of a bow and arrow, for the 1992 Olympic Park. Equally striking and first-rate was the contribution made by top model Nadja Auermann. The fashion star, on her way to make-up, briefly – but with expert authority – sums up the quality of the collection on the nine clothes stands: "Fantastic pieces".

This can certainly be said of the top later presented by Nadja Auermann: "Pole Position" is written in blue Swarovski stones across the front – one name, one range, both so good that she also wore the top at a private function in the drivers' area four weeks later at the Monaco Grand Prix.

Back to Barcelona: There are stars on the stage and stars in front of the stage. The BMW WilliamsF1 Team colours are first represented by drivers Juan Pablo Montoya and Marc Gené. BMW Motorsport Director Dr Mario Theissen is naturally also involved. He openly confesses: "Of course, when I'm at the racetrack I wear the official team clothing. But in all honesty, I frequently wear clothes from the collection in my free time."

The BMW WilliamsF1 Team is in a relaxed atmosphere – the entire evening is a party for the media. The trade press, lifestyle magazines and television are all represented and are using the opportunity to enquire about the fashion collection rather than about the set up, handling characteristics and rubber compounds. RTL reporter Kai Ebel, himself a lover of striking fashions, wants to find out from Juan Pablo just what the Montoya style is all about. Looking at his wife Connie, wearing an extremely elegant little black dress, the Colombian smiles: "My style is casual, cool and very relaxed."

These very qualities reflect his new collection, with which JPM is obviously very content: "The best ideas were put forward to me, and then I said what I liked and disliked. Connie's reaction proves that the collection is a massive hit: She loves the clothes and always wants me to bring parts of the collection back home."

The star performers of the BMW WilliamsF1 Team are accompanied this evening by celebrities from the world of show business and sport.

All are amazed by the 25-minute long presentation of the collection – a snazzy combination of sporting choreography, Spanish flamenco and artistic rollerblading. Everything is showcased on a small stage where every step and every turn made by the twelve models and four children is made to seem effortless, yet is the result of extremely precise coordination.

Everything goes according to plan, everything goes together well and everything continues in the same vivacious mood even after the presentation. 100 magnums of champagne are emptied.

Masterfully arranged finger food – from mini scampi skewers to mushroom ravioli – excites the palate. A live band gives an occasion for people to pack the dance floor. The organisers are clearly relieved to see the good atmosphere, the celebrity guests have long since been mixing with the other guests, and the invited media representatives are thoroughly enjoying the evening. Long after midnight, a roar of noise comes from the stage: "I love rock 'n roll" – backed by the singing of those on the dance floor. There's no doubt about it – it's party time . . .

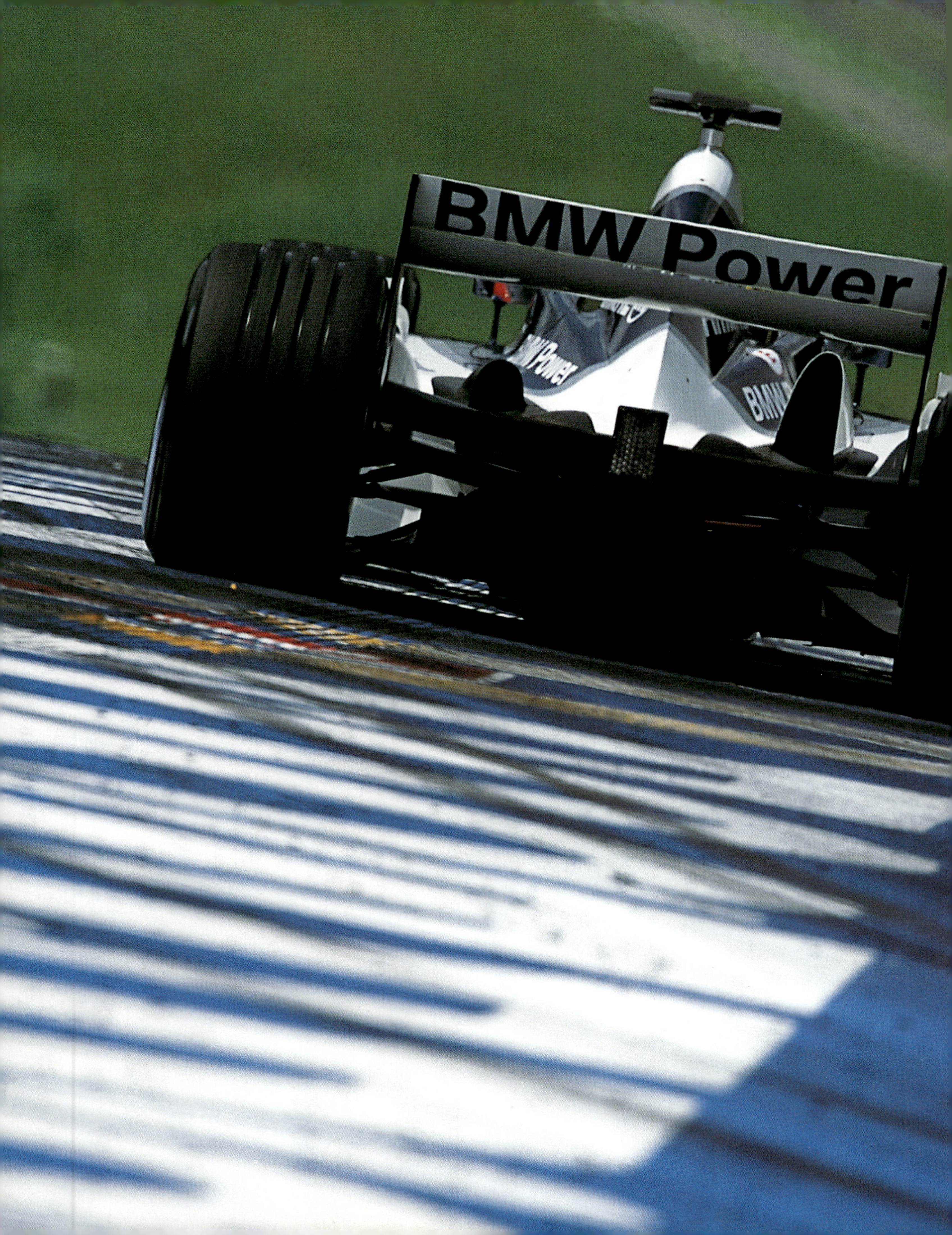
BMW Power
BMW Power

Results

1. Michael Schumacher
2. Kimi Räikkönen
3. Rubens Barrichello
4. Jenson Button
5. David Coulthard
6. **Ralf Schumacher**
7. Mark Webber
8. Jarno Trulli

GP Austria

Starting line-up: Flavio Briatore, head of sport at Renault, allows Fernando Alonso – who has only qualified for 19th position on the starting grid – to start the race from the pit lane.

1st start attempt: Cristiano da Matta's engine stalls and the Brazilian waves his arms – start cancelled.

2nd start attempt: Da Matta – now at the back of the starting grid – again experiences problems. The start is cancelled for a second time. Heinz-Harald Frentzen's Sauber is pushed into the pits with a clutch defect.

Start: Third time lucky! Michael Schumacher maintains his pole position. Juan Pablo Montoya passes Kimi Räikkönen and enters the first corner behind Michael Schumacher. Behind the Finn, Rubens Barrichello has edged past Nick Heidfeld. At the rear of the field, Jos Verstappen's Minardi rolls to a stop with a defective automatic choke control.

Lap 1: The Minardi cannot be rescued quickly enough from its dangerous position on the starting grid – the race marshals deploy the safety car.

Lap 2: First Olivier Panis, followed later by Justin Wilson, use this phase for refuelling.

Lap 5: The race is given the all-clear and resumes – Michael Schumacher leads ahead of Montoya, Räikkönen, Barrichello, Heidfeld, Antonio Pizzonia, Jarno Trulli, Jenson Button and Ralf Schumacher.

Lap 15: Ralf Schumacher makes his first pit stop, re-entering the race in eleventh position. Mark Webber completes a time penalty for unauthorised refuelling prior to the warm-up lap.

Lap 16: Light rain begins to fall over parts of the circuit. Michael Schumacher deviates from the ideal line. His lead over Montoya and Räikkönen reduces visibly.

Lap 18: The rain showers have passed, and Michael Schumacher is immediately able to improve his lap times.

Lap 20: Montoya, in second place, refuels and re-enters the race in sixth position.

Lap 21: Barrichello's refuelling stop goes wrong because of problems with the refuelling equipment. The Brazilian is stopped for 19.8 seconds.

Lap 22: Michael Schumacher extends his lead ahead of Räikkönen to 9.4 seconds.

Lap 23: The first three drivers – Michael Schumacher, Räikkönen, Button – come into the pits. During Michael Schumacher's refuelling stop, petrol on the neck of the refuelling pipe ignites. The Ferrari team has the presence of mind to extinguish the fire immediately, whilst Michael Schumacher remains seated in the car. The race is now led by Montoya, followed by Räikkönen.

Lap 32: A defective pressure compensation valve results in a leak in the BMW's engine cooling system, spelling the end of the race for Montoya, who up until that point was leading. Almost simultaneously, Michael Schumacher overtakes Räikkönen to take the lead of the race.

Lap 35: Barrichello pushes Button from third place.

Lap 41: A succession of quick lap times puts Michael Schumacher over eight seconds ahead of Räikkönen.

Lap 42: Everything goes to plan for Michael Schumacher's second pit stop. Räikkönen takes the lead for the time being.

Lap 43: Ralf Schumacher's pit stop causes him to drop from fifth to seventh position.

Lap 44: Fernando Alonso quits the race on the first bend due to engine trouble. The oil left behind on the track by his car causes difficulty for several drivers.

Lap 50: After Räikkönen and Barrichello have made their pit stop, Michael Schumacher retakes the lead.

Lap 57: Ralf Schumacher briefly leaves the track. David Coulthard takes advantage of this fact to push through into fifth position.

Lap 66: Barrichello tries everything possible to get past Räikkönen – but his efforts prove futile.

Lap 69: Michael Schumacher wins the race, which has been shortened by two laps. Räikkönen remains ahead of Barrichello and retains his leading position in the World Championship ranking. Button crosses the finishing line fourth, ahead of Coulthard and Ralf Schumacher.

accenture
Allianz
MICHELIN
NiQuitinCQ
NiQuitinCQ
ETROBRAS
castrol

Felix Austria

You can take away the Grand Prix from a country like Austria – but not its significance to Formula One.

A sense of nostalgia hangs over the A1-Ring. A small region, characterised by even smaller villages such as Judenburg and Knittelfeld, is saying goodbye to the chic world of elite racing having been banished from the 2004 racing calendar. The A1-Ring, Austria-Ring, airport races in Zeltweg – since 1964, Styria has always had a place in the Grand Prix calendar. This is the place where Bandini and Ickx triumphed. This is where Brambilla, Watson, Jones and de Angelis celebrated their first victories. This is where Lauda, Prost and Michael Schumacher won hard battles on the way to taking the World Championship title. Yet all this has to come to an end. Following the Belgian Grand Prix, the Austrian Grand Prix is also to set a warning example. This has been brought about on the one hand by a European-wide ban on tobacco advertising which is to come into effect on 31 July 2005, and on the other hand by a line of exotic countries waiting to join the Formula One club. Out of Europe and into the big, wide world!

However: Even if Formula One races are no longer held in Austria, it does not mean that Austria will have no place in the world of Formula One. On the contrary: The presence of this country with eight million inhabitants in elite racing will be like that of a super power.

If a major television station such as RTL requires an expert, the Austrian Niki Lauda will be in the front row. The Bahrain Grand Prix needs to be organised? Everybody is already recommending the Austrian Hans Geist. The Chinese Grand Prix in Shanghai needs appropriate security monitoring? A job for Austrian-based CAM, which incorporates Christof Ammann Management – the company entrusted by Bernie Ecclestone with international ticket sales.

A Formula One team is looking for a visionary major sponsor? It will presumably approach the head of Red Bull, Austrian Dietrich Mateschitz. Formula One is hungry? Ecclestone and his "Allsport" company come up with a suggestion: Paddock Club maestro Attila Dogudan and his Austrian catering firm Do&CO are at hand with their wooden spoons. A team boss is unhappy with the fitness of his drivers? A call to the Austrian physiotherapists is all it takes to get the sweat dripping. Erwin Göllner, Jo Leberer, Andy Kos, Daniel Dobringer: When a muscle needs a massage, Austrians are on the job.

If BMW wants to pamper guests with culinary delights, the Austrian "Joschi" Walch opens the doors to BMW Hospitality. And if Bernie Ecclestone is the host in the drivers' enclosure, he does so exclusively in the VIP area of the Austrian Karl Heinz Zimmermann.

Austria – a country whose history extends to the present day. Jochen Rindt, Niki Lauda, Gerhard Berger – there has hardly ever been a decade in elite racing which has not been decisively influenced and shaped by an Austrian front runner. These names must be mentioned if the current importance of Austrians in Formula One is to be explained. The spectacular career of Graz-born Jochen Rindt was without a doubt the "big bang" in the small Alpine republic as far as motor sport is concerned. Following in Rindt's wake, his fellow countrymen such as the journalists Helmut Zwickl and Heinz Prüller found their way into the Formula One drivers' enclosure. They did an awful lot on their part to support their fellow countrymen.

Jochen Rindt and Bernie Ecclestone were like twins where sport and business were concerned. The two would certainly have still been partners today, had Rindt's tragic accident in Monza not suddenly ended everything. "From this friendship alone, I can understand Bernie's obvious affinity towards Austrians", speculates Lauda. He also made a contribution to keep the red and white colours of the Austrian flag flying high in the drivers' enclosure. It was with Lauda that fitness considerations gained a foothold in Formula One. He was inspired by the teachings of Willy Dungl, which are still implemented by his pupils today.

Networks and connections are important in a hectic world of business in which one has to be able to rely on others. "Austrian specialness" alone is not enough. One person who knows that a lot more maintains the role of Austrians in Formula One is the new manager of the Formula One circuit in Bahrain, Hans Geist: "The Austrian temperament plays a role in our Formula One success. We are a mixture of Slavic, Italian, Czech and German cultures. That maybe makes us slightly more flexible. Mix that with a bit of Austrian trickery and all doors are open to us."

The turbo party

Past successes often determine aspirations and obligations for the future, as well as providing good cause to celebrate their anniversaries.

With something to celebrate, it had to look exactly as it did. The location – a 17th century castle, filled with admired Canalettos and Van Dycks. To ensure the event is in keeping with its station, approximately 20 square miles of the finest parkland are available, which is also host to a garden party. What's more, to ensure a truly exuberant party, the closest circle of friends has been extended to include around 150,000 guests.

Admittedly, the whole thing sounds rather extravagant, but it can be arranged – provided there is a milestone in sporting automobile history to celebrate. In addition to bearing the good name of the Earl of March, son of the tenth Duke of Richmond, the party will feature the family castle, Goodwood House, its vast estate and half of England's automobile community standing in the front garden. BMW really does have something to celebrate – something which will turn heads even in the most discerning of noble circles: The 20th anniversary of the first Formula One title won by the Brazilian Nelson Piquet. After only 630 days in Formula One, a BMW driven victory was achieved in 1983 at the last race of the season at the South African Grand Prix in Kyalami. Even then it was a significant triumph, for this was the first title won using turbo technology in the history of elite racing.

The main players from that time still read like the Who's Who of today's Grand Prix scene: Bernie Ecclestone and the members of his Brabham team, Herbie Blash, Charles Whiting and Gordon Murray. From BMW there is Paul Rosche, still a modern-day legend known as "Camshaft Paul". They all were, and indeed still are, behind the car which brought their success – the Brabham BT 52B BMW. Similar to an arrowhead, this thin, carbon fibre car was powered by a BMW four-cylinder engine which, thanks to turbocharger technology, electronic ignition and fuel injection systems, can produce a devilish 1,350 hp depending on the boost pressure. With its blue and white paintwork, side-mounted radiators and stub wings giving it the appearance of a missile, the car remains a work of art even today – 20 years later. BMW Motorsport Director, Dr Mario Theissen, looks at the BT52 and enthuses: "For me, it's the most beautiful Formula One car of them all. Even today."

BMW in Munich decided that this BT 52B BMW – the very car that won the 1983 race in Kyalami, and preferably with Nelson Piquet behind the wheel – should be one of the main attractions at the "Goodwood Festival of Speed".

As a public celebration of motor sport tradition, this festival has for years been the greatest event worldwide: Three carefree days spent admiring an array of vintage racing cars, attracting up to 150,000 spectators on the Earl's vast estate. The emphasis of this event is not just on "festival", it also focuses in particular on "speed". At Goodwood, cars of ages past are not just showcased to an interested public on the stage; here they are raced around a 1.16-mile long circuit lined with thousands of hay bails. This means that 20 years after its last outing, the BT 52B BMW has to be once again made fit to race.

Owing to its significance in the history of the company, the car was acquired from Bernie Ecclestone in 1996 and lovingly restored over two years to its original condition. Yet restoring a car and driving it at racing speeds are two different things, particularly since a mere four weeks preparation time was available.

The BT 52B BMW was taken from the Mobile Tradition museum to the men under the supervision of BMW Motorsport Director Dr Theissen. They immediately set to work. The fuel tank and brakes were given particular attention – safety first! Furthermore, the engine was dismantled, all the bearings were examined and finally all the main parts were completely taken apart.

Michelin – tyre supplier to BMW both then and now – showed its generosity and manufactured a couple of sets of slicks especially for the Sunday race at Goodwood. After all, the museum piece had up until now sat on the original tyres from the Kyalami race – as is befitting of a vintage car with such historical significance – and the rubber had turned as hard as stone.

New tyres were, however, one of the easier challenges to overcome. Obtaining the required special fuel proved a great deal harder. Today, the mention of the fuel makes Paul Rosche smile just as he did back then: "A friend kept a fuel mixture in his cellar for fighter planes from the war. This fuel worked marvellously in the turbo engine."

200 litres of this magic fuel had to be prepared for Goodwood. A search then had to be initiated for a specific type of 8V battery which has not been available in this size for many years, and without which the 1983 electronics in the BMW engine would not function.

Everything worked. Yet, true to the style of the company, the maxim is "play it safe". On 30 June at 6.30 p.m. sharp, the winning car was started for a test run at Landsberg airport – all in the experienced hands of Marc Surer. Surer, who drove for the Brabham BMW Team in his days as an active racing driver, is in his element: "I sat in the car for three hours – a lot of fine tuning was needed. Most importantly, we have programmed the computer chips."

The following day, a report can be sent to Rosche and Theissen: "Everything is in order, the equipment is complete." The only thing left to do is fly the car with an operations manager to England and to invite as many of the former team as possible to the party.

At Goodwood House, the Egyptian room has been reserved especially. The room is a good four metres high with dark oak parquet flooring, ancient oil paintings and varnished, gold-trimmed walls. Numerous salmon dishes are on offer, as well as finest lamb, chilled white wine and a fine red – it only takes a few minutes for the memories to come flooding back. Piquet for example, who was always telling jokes until just before the race started. "Dreadful jokes which cannot be repeated", as he himself says. Or how Piquet suddenly came into the pits in the middle of a race, whereupon the mechanics wildly set to work on the Brabham, changed the tyres, refuelled – yet amid the chaos, nobody had realised that Piquet had long since got out of the car because of a technical defect. The car was ready, but it did not drive away because there was no-one in the car to drive it away…

Gordon Murray, the then chassis constructor, is in a generous mood. In a brief eulogy, he praises BMW and Rosche: "Everyone who takes a look back at the '83 season thinks that this car was tremendously highly developed from a technical point of view. Yet this could not be further from the truth – in fact, the very opposite was the case. The BT 52 is perhaps the simplest Formula One car to ever win a Grand Prix. There has not been a car in the history of Formula One which required as little tuning as this one – ask the mechanics! The new regulations prohibited so many aerodynamic aids that it became clear to us that the season could only be won by using engine power alone. And, my dear Paul, we were right."

Such compliments make "Camshaft Paul" feel truly sentimental. With today in mind, he emphasises: "It could be seen back then that the Bavarians and English belong together – and I am still friends with Gordon today." However, this hippy with long hair and small, round sunglasses did not always make life easy for him. Rosche cannot help laughing even today: "We both had a meeting with the Board of Directors. I was impressed when Gordon got into the lift next to me in BMW's "Four Cylinder" building. He was dressed smartly – appropriate for the occasion, but not in his usual style – wearing a buttoned-up suit, nice tie, everything was perfect. Then I looked down and could not believe my eyes. In addition to the suit and tie, Gordon was wearing plastic sandals – without any socks."

Although this all happened 20 years ago, it seems like it happened yesterday. Just like Piquet's 14-point deficit three races before the finale. For many people it is still beyond belief how he managed to turn the 1983 season around. Piquet all too willingly tells the story this evening: "I was testing in Monza. Paul arrived three or four hours prior to the test carrying a small wheel from the turbo charger in his pocket. 'We must try this out – it's been made especially for us', he said. The moment the part was fitted, the turbo "slump" that we had endured throughout the season almost vanished. The engine was perfect.

I immediately said: Now we'll win the World Championship – easily."

No sooner said than done. Beaming, laughing faces, spellbound by memories both then and today. Herbie Blash raises his glass to the current BMW Motorsport Director: "Mario, I know that you were not there at the time, but this is a very emotional evening, and I would like to say thank you on behalf of us all."

In the past it was a triumph, today it is history, which is always the aspiration and obligation for tomorrow. Theissen takes up Blash's words, moving away from the past to concentrate on BMW's current commitment to Formula One: "There is a huge difference between then and now. Then we won the title, now we must try everything in order to win it. I can, however, promise you one thing – we are giving everything we've got to once again achieve our aim."

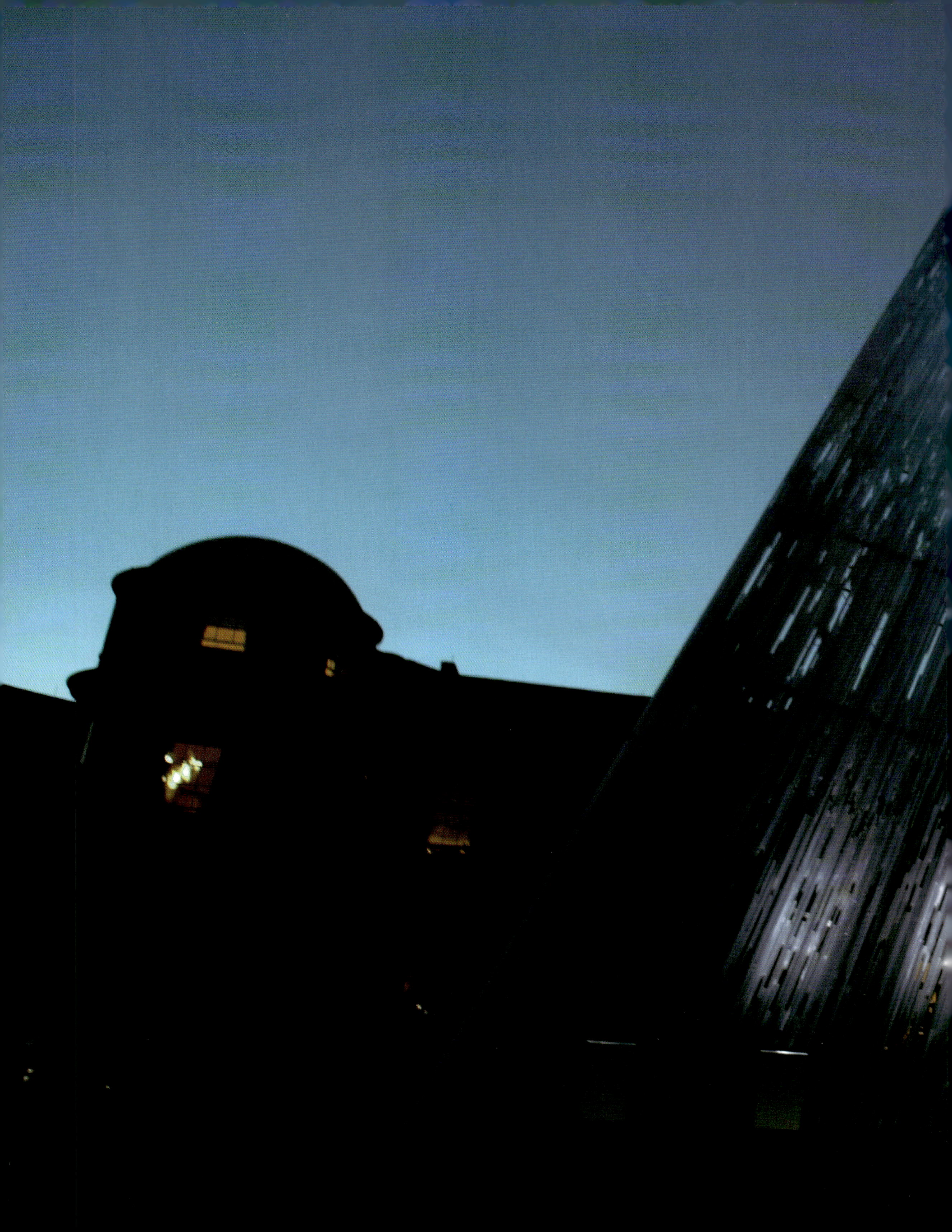

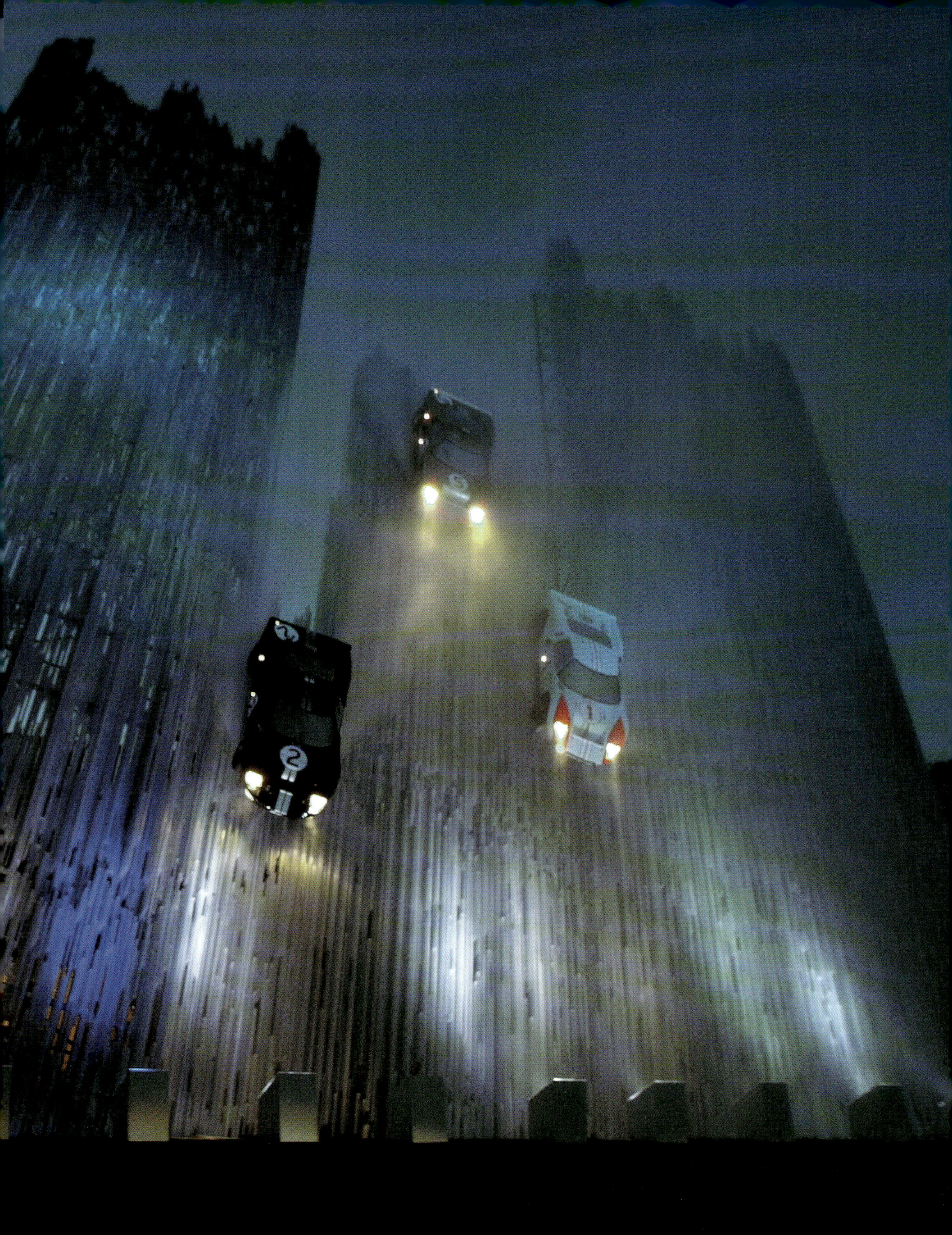

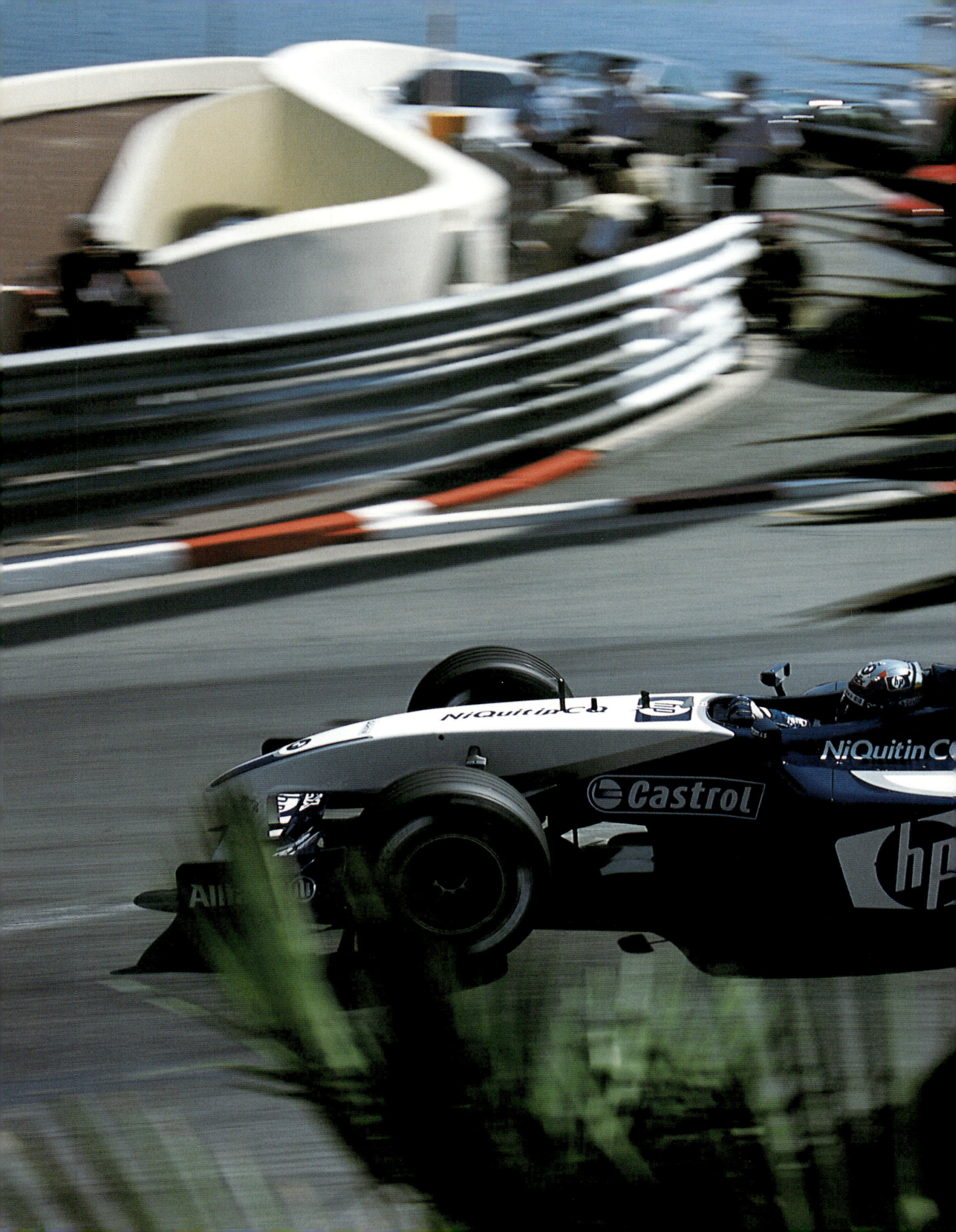
NiQuitin CQ
Castrol
NiQuitin CQ
hp

GP Monaco

Results

1. **Juan Pablo Montoya**
2. Kimi Räikkönen
3. Michael Schumacher
4. **Ralf Schumacher**
5. Fernando Alonso
6. Jarno Trulli
7. David Coulthard
8. Rubens Barrichello

Start: For the first time this season, BMW has a driver in pole position, with Ralf Schumacher. Ralf Schumacher is able to defend his pole position from the moment the race gets underway. His neighbour in the first row, Kimi Räikkönen, blocks a full-on attack from Jarno Trulli, thereby allowing Juan Pablo Montoya to take second place. After the first bend, known as St. Devote, these four drivers are followed by Michael Schumacher, Fernando Alonso, David Coulthard and Rubens Barrichello.

Lap 1: Coming out of the new chicane situated by the port, Heinz-Harald Frentzen careens into the crash barrier with such force that the safety car is deployed. Before the safety car phase, Ralf Schumacher had a 2.2-second advantage over his team mate, which has now been erased.

Lap 5: The race gets under way once again. As is typical for Monaco, the leading positions remain unchanged until the time comes for the first refuelling stops to be made: Ralf Schumacher leads ahead of Montoya, Räikkönen, Trulli, Michael Schumacher, Alonso and Coulthard.

Lap 19: Montoya closes the gap between himself and the race leader, Ralf Schumacher. For the first time, there is less than a second separating the two.

Lap 20: Montoya is now only a few tenths of a second behind his team mate and heightens the pressure.

Lap 21: Ralf Schumacher is the first of the race leaders to enter the pits for refuelling.

Lap 22: Montoya makes the most of the clear track ahead of him to complete the fastest lap time until that moment.

Lap 23: Montoya, now leading the race, comes into the pits. After 8.2 seconds he returns to the race in seventh position ahead of his team mate.

Lap 25: Räikkönen, who is leading ahead of Trulli and Michael Schumacher by almost ten seconds, comes into the pits. Michael Schumacher is hot on Trulli's heels, but he is unable to overtake the Italian on the narrow city street circuit.

Lap 27: With Trulli in the pits, Michael Schumacher assumes the lead for the first time in the race.

Lap 32: After Michael Schumacher's pit stop in the previous lap, the positions are as follows: Montoya leads ahead of Räikkönen, Michael and Ralf Schumacher, Trulli, Coulthard, Alonso and Barrichello. The first refuelling stop has the most adverse effect on Ralf Schumacher, who falls from first to fourth position. His brother has benefited most from his pit stop, which was relatively late in comparison with the other leading drivers, moving up from fifth to third place.

Lap 39: With half of the race complete, the positions are as before: Montoya leads ahead of Räikkönen, Michael and Ralf Schumacher.

Lap 53: Ralf Schumacher skids off the track at the Rascasse. He loses about ten seconds but is able to continue the race.

Lap 62: Once the second round of refuelling stops has come to an end, the line-up at the front of the race has a familiar feel: Montoya leads ahead of Räikkönen, Michael and Ralf Schumacher. Alonso is able to push past Trulli and Coulthard.

Lap 75: Räikkönen narrows the time between him and Montoya to 0.5 seconds.

Lap 78: Räikkönen is unable to force Montoya into making a single mistake, and Montoya wins his second Grand Prix. Michael Schumacher crosses the line in third place, followed by his brother Ralf, Alonso, Trulli, Coulthard and Barrichello.

Light at the end of the tunnel

Montoya has long been waiting for a victory. Just like his team, for which better times are finally on the horizon.

It is the Prince's honour: On his right, Prince Albert, and on his left, Caroline of Monaco. Patrick Head, Technical Director at WilliamsF1, is also in the Prince's box, joined of course by the two rival racers Kimi Räikkönen and Michael Schumacher. The protagonist, however, stands in the middle of this top-calibre phalanx: Juan Pablo Montoya, winner of the 61st Monaco Grand Prix. Visibly moved, and with tears in his eyes, he listens to the sounds of the Colombian national anthem.

The fact that Montoya is standing at the top of the podium seems a minor miracle to many motor sport insiders. Certainly, the street circuit in the principality is the only track in the world with a tunnel. It is therefore predestined to show everybody that there is always light at the end of the tunnel. Yet the signs could not have been any worse. Montoya had not had a single victory in nearly one and a half years. Furthermore, as BMW Motorsport Director Dr Mario Theissen openly admits, "the season got off to a bad start" for the BMW WilliamsF1 Team.

To top it all off, the Monaco track is certainly not the preferred course of the BMW WilliamsF1 Team. On this subject, Dr Theissen says: "Apart from last year, we have previously not been in good form at this race." In actual fact, BMW has never won a race in Monaco, and the last time WilliamsF1 claimed victory at the track was exactly 20 years ago. Why, then, should Juan Pablo Montoya have great expectations at the Monaco Grand Prix?

He is all the more relieved after the race: "Victory here is really more exciting for me than my success in the Indy 500 three years ago. It's a really important victory, both for me and the entire team."

Winning the Monaco Grand Prix is really a milestone for Montoya. His first and last victory in Formula One took place in September 2001. In the turbulent world of Formula One, that is a long time. Montoya says: "I never thought that it would take me more time to win my second Formula One race than it did to win my first."

Without doubt, the Colombian – followed by his high-spirited wife – is an unmissable highlight amongst the world's leading racing drivers. He is a racer through and through as his boss and former racing driver Gerhard Berger recognises without envy: "Juan simply meets your expectations of what you want a racing driver to be. With regard to status, image and driving style. He arouses emotions in people."

These, however, are emotions which can easily change. Achieving seven poles in quick succession in the previous season is something to be proud of. But seven pole position starts also contain an element of danger, especially when these pole positions are not associated with victories. The horrible term "Training World Champion" is coined.

Speaking after his victory in Monaco, Montoya says: "I must admit that I often thought that I had some sort of curse on me. I have been so close to victory so many times and then something prevented me from actually achieving that victory. Either my luck had run out or something broke or went wrong."

In Monaco, Montoya and his team did not make a single mistake. The part of the race after the second tyre change was Gerhard Berger's particular favourite: "Juan knew that Räikkönen could stay out on the track for perhaps two, three or four laps longer. He also knew how fast the Finn can drive, and he was aware that every split second would

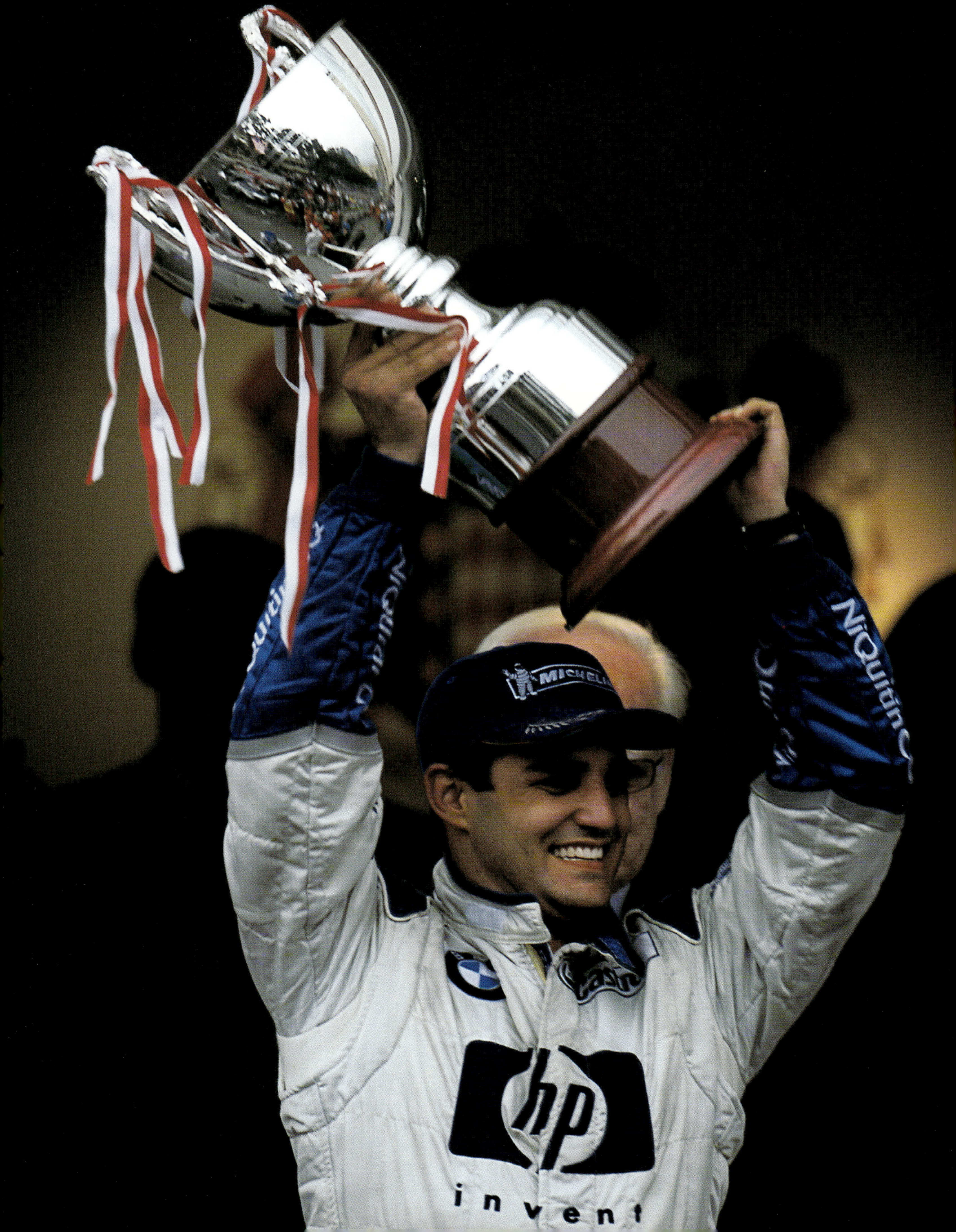
hp
invent

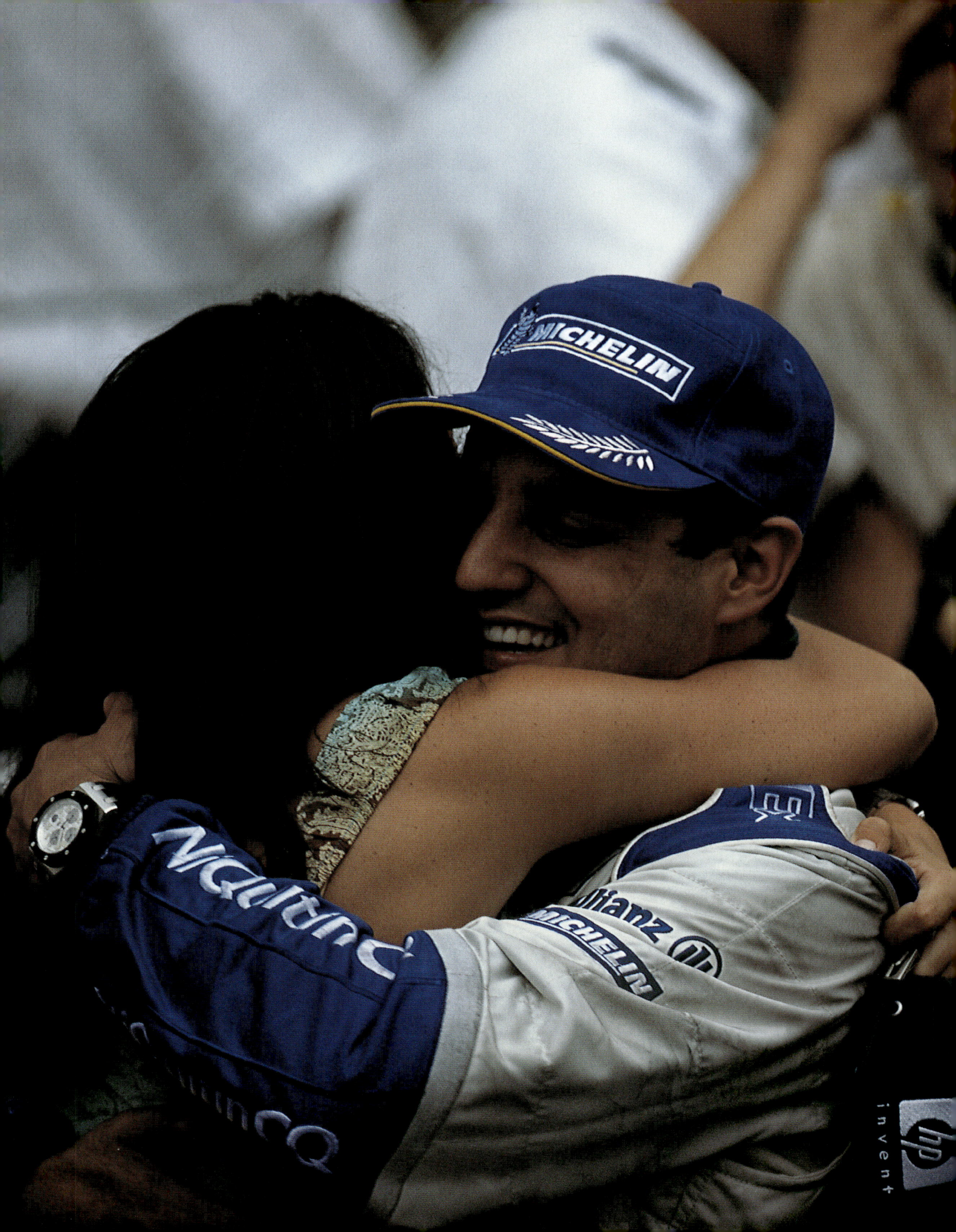
MICHELIN
MICHELIN
invent

count. However, Juan didn't make a single mistake when driving into the pits. He positioned the car neatly, the team carried out a quick pit stop and that enabled him to come out in front. And that was it."

Even Patrick Head, not normally a man to offer many words of praise, is delighted: "This is an extremely important and deserved victory. It was such a testing race. There wasn't a moment in which you could relax. It was a fight to the very end." So was it a race which was tailored to a high-spirited Latino fighter such as Montoya? Head laughs: "Juan thinks that all races are made for him…"

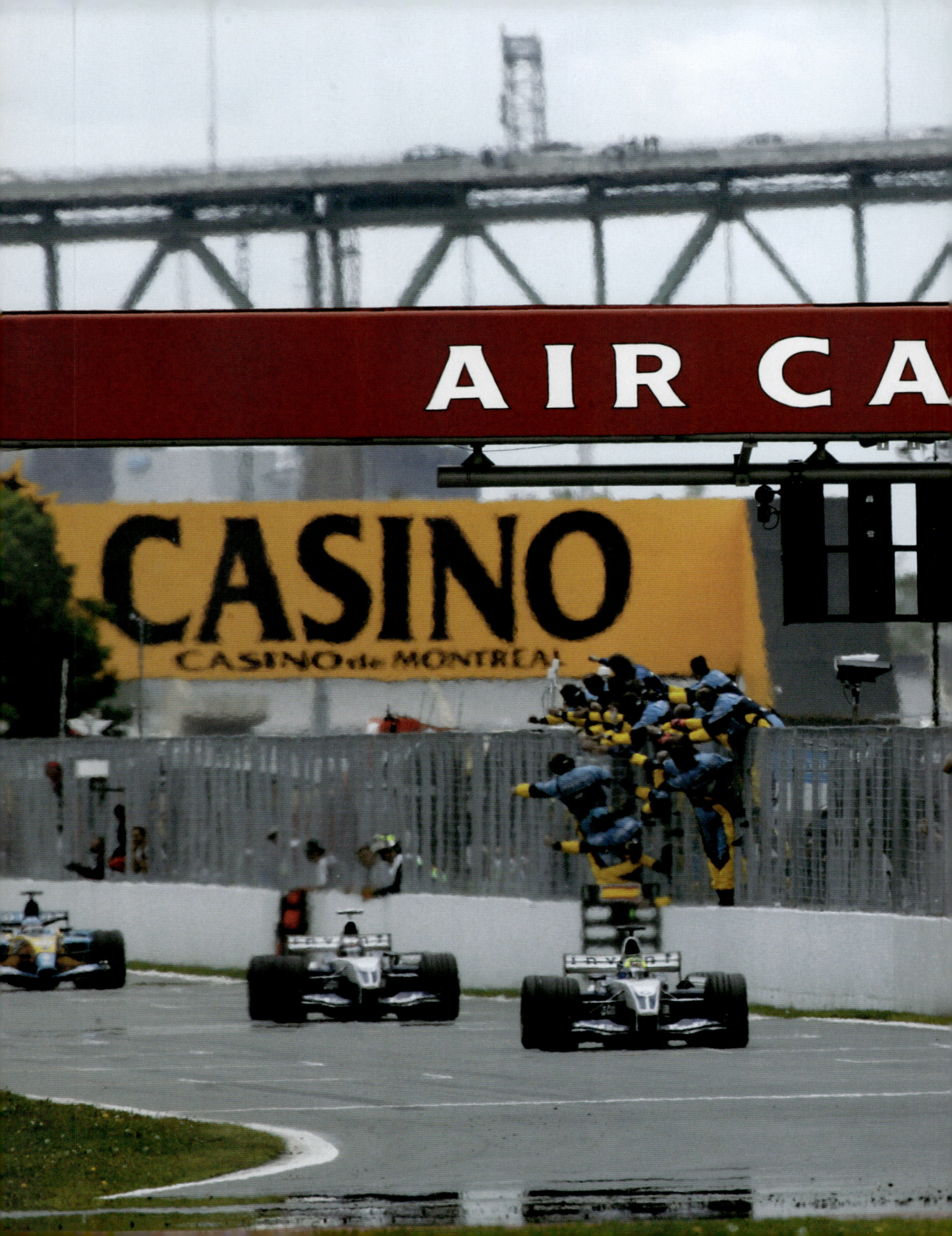
AIR CA
CASINO
CASINO de MONTREAL

Results

1. Michael Schumacher
2. **Ralf Schumacher**
3. **Juan Pablo Montoya**
4. Fernando Alonso
5. Rubens Barrichello
6. Kimi Räikkönen
7. Mark Webber
8. Olivier Panis

GP Canada

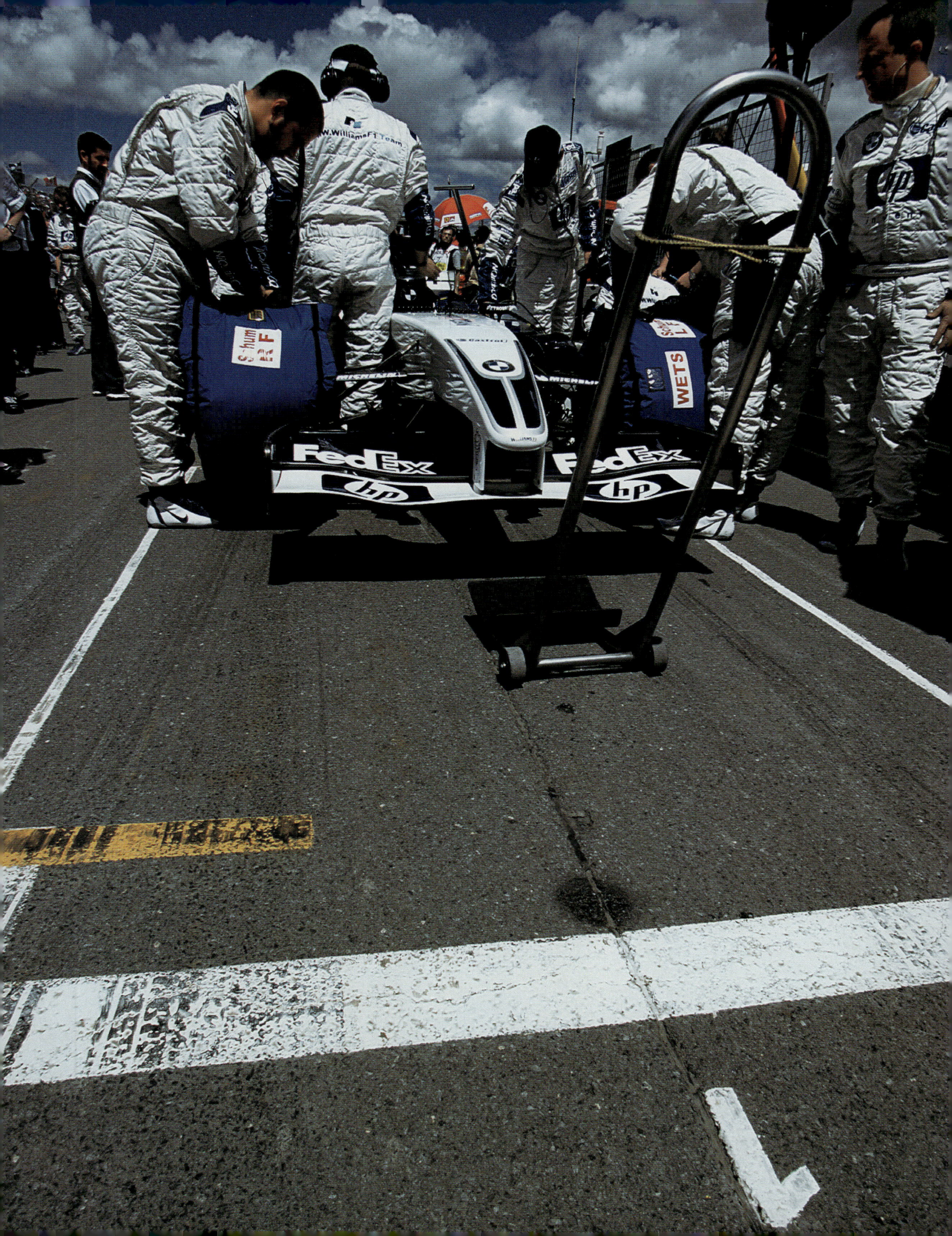
FedEx
FedEx
hp
hp
WETS

Starting line-up: Following an accident in final training, Kimi Räikkönen takes last position for the start, but instead prefers to start from the pit lane. The refuelling ban between qualifying and the actual race is not applicable in this circumstance. The Finn takes on board plenty of fuel and races – in contrast to his direct competitors – with a one-stop strategy.

Start: Ralf Schumacher immediately converts his pole position into leadership of the race. Team mate Juan Pablo Montoya is equally able to defend his second place against any challenge from Michael Schumacher. Rubens Barrichello clips the tail of Fernando Alonso's car and in doing so destroys his front wing.

Lap 1: Antonio Pizzonia miscalculates his offensive on David Coulthard and Jarno Trulli in the hairpin bend, hitting the tail of the Italian's car.

Lap 2: Montoya spins when coming out of the last corner ahead of the finishing straight and drops behind Michael Schumacher, Alonso and Mark Webber into fifth position. Barrichello and Trulli come into the pits for repairs.

Lap 10: After Montoya successfully overtakes Webber, he now pushes Alonso out of third place. Meanwhile, Michael Schumacher is increasing the pressure on his brother, who is struggling with worn tyres.

Lap 15: No change at the front of the race: Ralf Schumacher leads ahead of his brother Michael, followed some way behind by Montoya, Alonso and Webber.

Lap 16: Michael Schumacher experiences initial problems with worn brakes.

Lap 20: One lap after his team mate, Ralf Schumacher enters the pits for refuelling. Ralf Schumacher decides not to change the front tyres. His brother Michael takes the lead, and both Jordans drop out of the race owing to technical problems.

Lap 21: Michael Schumacher enters the pits. Although at 10.6 seconds, his stop is 1.8 seconds longer than that of his brother, he re-enters the race ahead of Ralf Schumacher.

Lap 26: After race leader Alonso has completed his refuelling stop, there is an established sequence at the front of the race: Michael Schumacher leads ahead of his brother, Montoya, Alonso, Räikkönen (who still has not had to refuel), Barrichello and Coulthard.

Lap 33: Whilst travelling at 340 km/h, the rear right tyre on Räikkönen's McLaren bursts. The Finn manages to get his car under control and immediately heads for the pits.

Lap 48: Two laps after Montoya and one lap after Ralf Schumacher, Michael Schumacher enters the pits. The Ferrari driver re-enters the race behind the leader, Alonso, but ahead of the two BMW WilliamsF1 Team drivers.

Lap 47: Coulthard abandons the race due to gearbox problems.

Lap 48: After the early departure from the race of Heinz-Harald Frentzen – his electronics packed up – the second Sauber driver, Nick Heidfeld, quits the race because of engine trouble.

Lap 55: Race leader Alonso enters the pits and re-enters the race in fourth position.

Lap 64: Ralf Schumacher is obviously able to drive faster than his brother, who is just ahead of him, but he has no opportunity to overtake the Ferrari. Montoya and Alonso close the gap rapidly from behind, yet none of them dares overtake.

Lap 70: The first four – Michael Schumacher ahead of Ralf Schumacher, Montoya and Alonso – cross the finishing line only 4.4 seconds apart. Considerably further behind, Barrichello, Räikkönen, Webber and Olivier Panis cross the line and qualify for points.

Always neatly in line

Is there too little overtaking in Formula One? And if so, why? How could this be changed?

It took 50 laps, and for many these 50 laps were far too much. As harmonious as a pair of twins, Michael and Ralf Schumacher raced one behind the other following the first refuelling stop. This was fine for Michael, who won the race in this way. It was less pleasant for his brother Ralf, who started from pole position, but had to resign himself to second place during the race. After the winners' ceremony, Ralf Schumacher said: "I could have driven more quickly, but there was no way of passing Michael."

Many people took a different view. One of the accusations levied at Ralf Schumacher was that he had driven too defensively. Another accusation was that he especially wouldn't attack his brother. BMW Motorsport Director, Gerhard Berger, puts forward a different argument – based on the experience of 210 Grand Prix races: "Anyone who reproaches Ralf Schumacher for not overtaking his brother must also understand that Juan Pablo Montoya also followed behind Ralf for many laps without once trying to overtake him. Similarly, Fernando Alonso trailed Montoya without attempting to overtake."

Formula One and overtaking – this is a subject which for years has generated fierce discussion amongst drivers, technicians, sponsors and fans. Five-time World Champion, Michael Schumacher – who vehemently defended his brother after the race, saying "Ralf is not so stupid as to attempt showy extras or kamikaze stunts" – points out the problem with modern-day Formula One: "In Formula One, you can be a second quicker than the driver in front of you, yet there is sometimes no chance to overtake him. It makes no sense to even attempt to do so."

There are various reasons why the world's best drivers all too often complete laps of the course neatly in line. Marc Surer, a former Formula One racing driver and now a popular Grand Prix commentator, cites the most important: "Too short braking distances, 'dirty air' and anti-overtaking racetracks."

The Swiss commentator elucidates his arguments: "The main problem is the short braking distance. The braking process in modern-day Formula One is completed within a second – and at the very most, within two seconds. There is barely any scope for launching an attack during this limited time of braking deceleration."

According to Surer, a further problem is that "dirty air is still present. The front wings are still too sensitive to the air vortices caused by the car in front. This means that you can't drive hot on the heels of the car in front – the prerequisite for an overtaking manoeuvre."

Surer's third point of criticism: "Too few circuits display a profile like Indy 500 tracks, for example. Here, you have to race along the curved infield with raised wings, which then produce an outstanding slipstream for overtaking on the long straights."

When the catchword "circuit" is mentioned, the globally active racetrack architect Hermann Tilke makes his voice heard. His theory: "Modern day Formula One drivers are too good. They no longer make mistakes." Tilke's conclusion: "Incorporate bends in which drivers are 20-30% likely to make mistakes." Tilke continues: "If this were the case, they wouldn't be able to accelerate out of the bend perfectly. They would then be lacking this small advantage on the subsequent straight, allowing the car behind to overtake at the next bend." Patrick Head, Technical Director at WilliamsF1, also understands the phenomenon of rare driving errors – even if his understanding is more from a technical viewpoint: "There were times when drivers had brakes which were often unable to endure an entire Grand Prix distance. They therefore had to be careful when using the brakes. Drivers had gearboxes in which gears would regularly fail. Furthermore, the tyres deteriorated towards the end of the race. All of this created opportunities for overtaking."

So, is it best to return to the "good old days"? Or could the lack of overtaking manoeuvres be overrated? Are Formula One audiences – as opposed to American NASCAR and Indy Sport audiences – not as obsessed solely with close duels for a certain position? Are they instead more interested in technical, tactical and strategic great feats achieved by a driver working in conjunction with his team?

Two men who have pervaded Formula One like nobody else have not unreservedly joined in the general call for more overtaking opportunities: Bernie Ecclestone and Max Mosley. Representing both men, FIA President Mosley formulates his opinion: "Whoever truly believes that Formula One fans only get their money's worth from overtaking manoeuvres is failing to understand the sport and its fans. Parallels can be drawn with football, where the focus is supposedly on countless goals alone. Even so, on a Saturday afternoon many fans still go home after the match in high spirits after seeing their team win an exciting game by a mere 1:0."

Allianz
Allianz
Allianz
Allianz
Allianz
MICHELIN
FedEx
Castrol
BMW
hp
Allianz
MICHELIN
MUMM

Results

1. **Ralf Schumacher**
2. **Juan Pablo Montoya**
3. Rubens Barrichello
4. Fernando Alonso
5. Michael Schumacher
6. Mark Webber
7. Jenson Button
8. Nick Heidfeld

GP Europe

Start: Kimi Räikkönen easily translates his pole position start into leadership of the race. His neighbour in the first row, Michael Schumacher, is out-accelerated on the dirty, inside part of the track by his brother Ralf. A similar thing happens to Juan Pablo Montoya, who is overtaken by Rubens Barrichello at the same time. The Colombian is immediately subjected to a fierce offensive from the two Renault drivers.

Lap 5: Räikkönen continuously extends his lead, which now stands at 4.8 seconds ahead of Ralf Schumacher. The two leading drivers are followed by Michael Schumacher, Barrichello, Montoya, Jarno Trulli, Fernando Alonso and Olivier Panis – all of whom will be awarded winners' points if they maintain their current positions.

Lap 9: Jacques Villeneuve, who has overtaken the two Minardis after a protracted struggle, spins out and falls back into last place. Nick Heidfeld, who started the race from the pit lane, also manages to push past the second Minardi.

Lap 11: Panis suffers brake problems and his car spins.

Lap 16: Räikkönen, who is 9.4 seconds ahead of Ralf Schumacher, and Michael Schumacher both come in for their first refuelling stop. For the first time in the race, Ralf Schumacher takes the lead. Räikkönen re-enters the race in sixth place, with Michael Schumacher in seventh place.

Lap 18: After Barrichello completed his pit stop in the previous lap, Montoya, Alonso and David Coulthard now all enter the pits at the same time.

Lap 22: Only now does Ralf Schumacher have to refuel. Returning to the track 7.7 seconds later in second place, he is 4.3 seconds behind Räikkönen, but ahead of his brother Michael, Barrichello, Montoya, Alonso and Trulli.

Lap 26: Räikkönen suffers engine trouble. Ralf Schumacher takes the lead ahead of his brother Michael and Barrichello.

Lap 35: Ralf Schumacher is in the lead – and his brother Michael is not presenting a threat. Barrichello is unable to keep up with the pace set by the two brothers. Furthermore, Barrichello is coming under increasing pressure from Montoya, who in turn is pursued by Alonso, Trulli and Coulthard.

Lap 37: Among the leading drivers, Michael Schumacher initiates the second pit stop phase one lap ahead of his team mate. Trulli is forced out of the race due to fuel pump problems, whilst Panis is forced to quit the race following a second spin.

Lap 41: During his second pit stop, lasting 8.3 seconds, Montoya is able to overtake Barrichello. Without the Brazilian in front, Montoya dramatically reduces the gap between him and Michael Schumacher in third place.

Lap 42: Despite making a pit stop, Ralf Schumacher is able to defend his lead.

Lap 43: Coulthard, until now in second place, has a very quick pit stop lasting only 6.5 seconds. At the same time, Montoya attacks Michael Schumacher from the outside in the Dunlop bend. Michael Schumacher resists and spins into the gravel, where he is pushed back onto the track by track marshals. This is allowed in the case of a driver being stranded in a dangerous position, provided that the engine is still running. Both were true in this case. As a result of the time lost, the Ferrari driver is now only in sixth place.

Lap 52: For several laps now, Coulthard has been piling the pressure on fourth-placed Alonso.

Lap 57: Cristiano da Matta's car is the second Toyota to leave the race – this time due to engine trouble.

Lap 58: Whilst braking into the NGK chicane, Coulthard is only able to avoid Alonso at the last second. The Scot, who later blames Alonso for braking too early, has a severe accident. Alonso, considering himself blameless, is able to carry on.

Lap 60: Ralf Schumacher wins his fifth Grand Prix. Montoya completes the double victory for the BMW WilliamsF1 Team.

The double victory

The best agreements are those in which both parties win. At the Nürburgring, there was a similar double victory to be celebrated between BMW and WilliamsF1.

Waiting pays off. After weeks and months of secretly conducted negotiations, the European Grand Prix finally provided the occasion for the group photograph: Chairman of the Board of BMW Group, Dr Helmut Panke, and Member of the Board of BMW AG, Development and Purchasing, Dr Burkhard Göschel, stand alongside WilliamsF1 Team owner Sir Frank Williams. Smiling behind the trio are the two BMW Motorsport Directors, Dr Mario Theissen and Gerhard Berger. The photograph shows winners together: Partners BMW and WilliamsF1 have agreed to work together for a further five years. The new agreement runs until the end of the season in 2009, and was concluded 18 months prior to the expiration of the current agreement.

The negotiations were conducted calmly: Both sides were self-confident, committed to the task and fair in their actions – and from an outside point of view acted with the utmost discretion.

At no time was any official information released about the negotiations – causing all the more media speculation as to the progression of the talks. You could read and listen to reports of completely contradictory scenarios – even including the separation of the two partners.

Theissen explains just exactly what the months of clarification entailed: "We intended to discover an optimised and more intensive form of cooperation between BMW and WilliamsF1."

Theissen expands on this, saying: "The crucial difference between the current and future cooperation between both companies now lies in the increased integration of the vast resources of luxury car manufacturer BMW and the special expertise of WilliamsF1, one of the most successful teams in the history of Formula One."

This settlement process was tiring – for months, up to a dozen specialists from both sides sat at the negotiating table and searched for the optimum settlement. The agenda contained the coordination of the two corporate cultures and the laying bare of cards. Furthermore, an extensive exchange of company secrets had to be conducted in a way that involved a fair distribution of give and take for both sides.

The fact that this has been achieved is confirmed by the Head of Development, Dr Göschel, at the Nürburgring: "This new agreement envisages the increased integration of both partners. As an automobile manufacturer, possibilities are open to us that a racing team would never have – and we have to exploit this potential together. Conversely, it is a question of supporting, using and optimally integrating the expert knowledge of one of the most important teams in the history of Formula One."

Williams, the team's boss, can only agree with this: "Since our collaboration began in 2000, BMW has been an extremely impressive and highly motivated engine partner. I am optimistic in every respect that the structure of our new agreement will allow us to profit more extensively from the possibilities open to BMW."

Theissen expands upon the objectives of the intensified collaboration: "The contractual negotiations were protracted, but we were happy to take our time and calmly elucidate every detail. From the very outset of its involvement in Formula One, it was a crucial criterion for BMW to fully use and increase the company's expertise. We therefore built our Formula One factory in Munich within shouting distance of our Research and Innovation Centre (FIZ). A comparable relationship between the Grove and Munich sites will be achieved in future using joint and general project management – thereby generating synergistic effects and optimising processes."

The specific significance of this is outlined by Theissen's view of the immediate future: "Within the framework of this enhanced cooperation, BMW will make a commitment beyond the development and construction of the engines. In the first phase, we are concentrating on the joint development of drive train transmission. Furthermore, the team will increasingly benefit from the simulation and experimental expertise of the Research and Innovation Centre."

An agreement and a glimpse of the immediate future – the European Grand Prix was ideal for both of these. The joint result at the Nürburgring showed everyone just what has been achieved by the BMW WilliamsF1 Team both on and off the track. A double victory in every sense of the word . . .

Background GP Europe

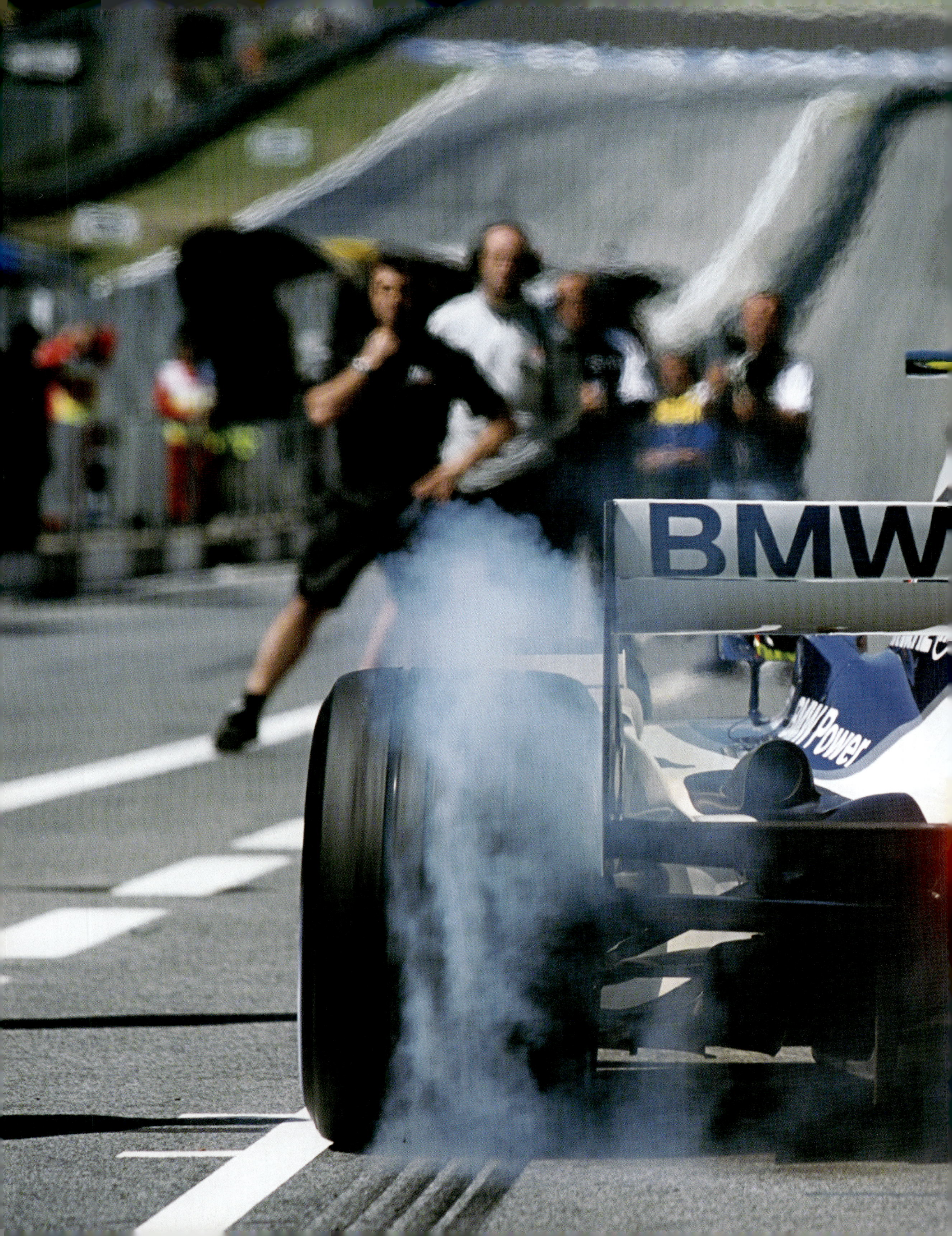
BMW
BMW Power

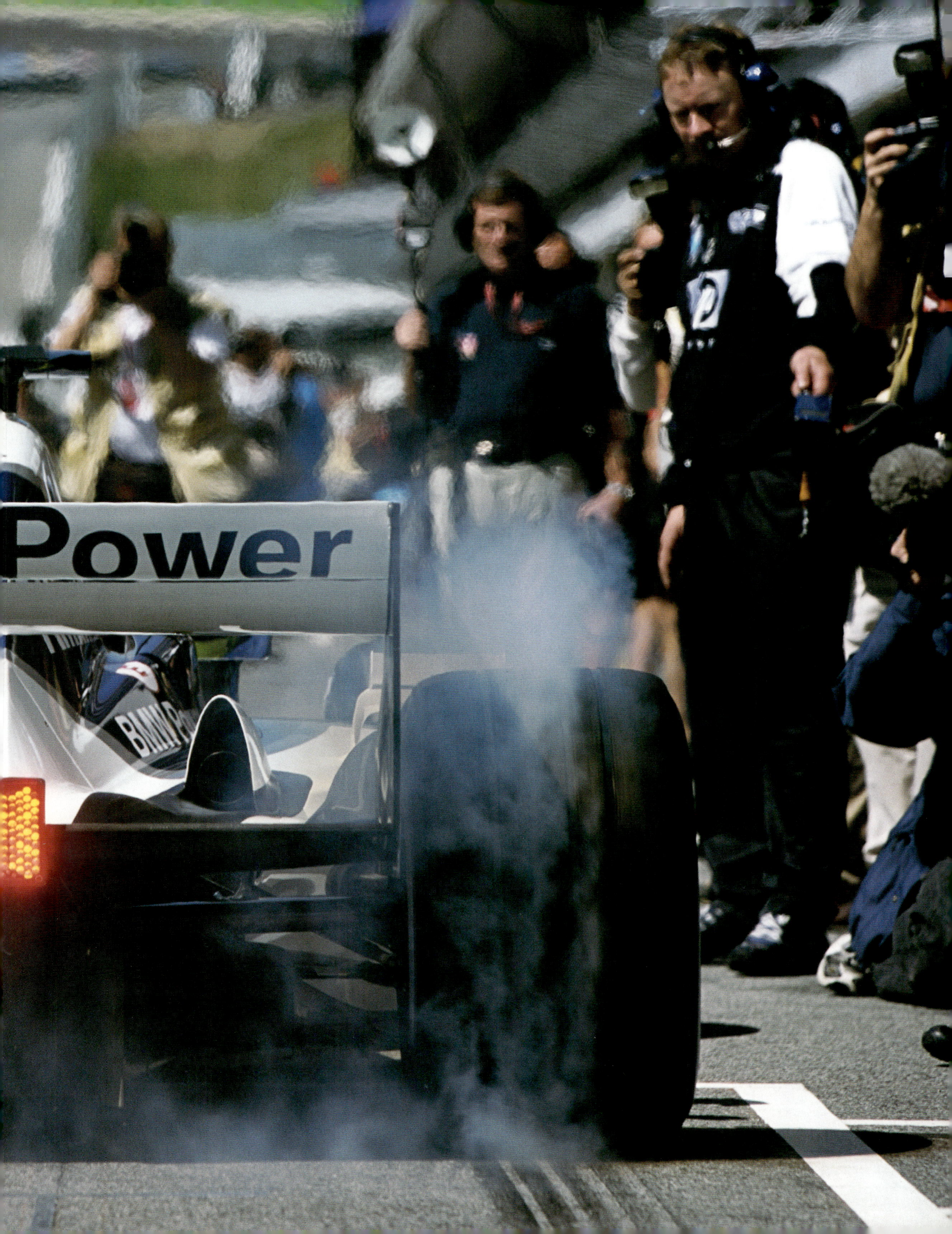
Power

Facts and Figures: BMW P83

- The BMW P83 delivers over 900 bhp.
- The engine can achieve a maximum of 19,200 rpm.
- For racing, the engine speed is limited to 19,000 rpm.
- The idling rev count is 4,000 rpm.
- The engine weighs less than 90 kilograms.
- The engine has a race life of 500 km before it requires inspection.
- A total of 200 units of the BMW P83 are built, with the team taking ten engines to each race.
- By the end of its service life, the engine will have undergone 1,388 further development measures.
- The engine features 1,000 different types of component. Each engine comprises approximately 5,000 component parts.
- The volume of intake air equates to 1,995 cubic metres per hour.
- The maximum piston acceleration is 10,000 g.
- The maximum piston speed is 40 metres per second; the average piston speed is 25 metres per second.
- Exhaust gases can reach 950 °C.
- The maximum air temperature in the pneumatic system is 250 °C.

BMW Pow

invent
FedEx
PETROBRAS
PETROBRAS
MICHELIN
MICHELIN
FedEx
FedEx

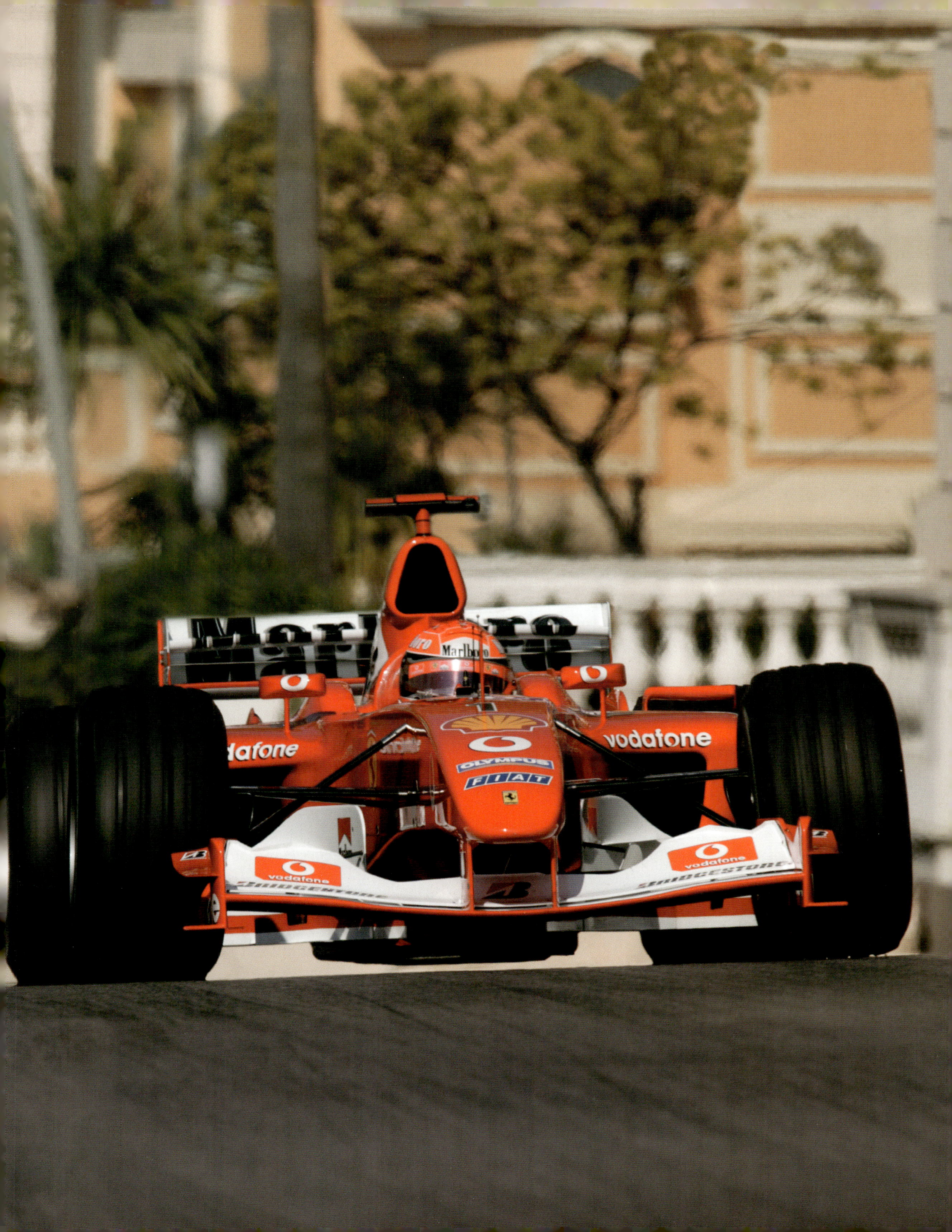
vodafone
OLYMPUS
FIAT
vodafone
vodafone

"The challenge remains…"

The laws of physics do not change – but the boundaries of technical possibilities do. A discussion with Dr Mario Theissen and Heinz Paschen.

Dr Theissen, after four years as BMW Motorsport Director, whom do you feel closer to today – the inventor of the petrol engine or a conductor such as Karajan?
MT: The task contains a bit of both elements, but of course neither element can describe it exactly. On the one hand, we are talking about technology and not music, that is to say that an engineer is required here. On the other hand, it's not me who develops the engine, it's Heinz Paschen and his team. My task focuses on the strategic direction and the operative control of BMW Motorsport. As far as that goes, I am more a conductor than an inventor.

In your position, how would you outline the tense relationship between "technician" and "head of an elite force"?
MT: It is my belief that a tense relationship mainly comes about when the boss is neither a technician nor an engineer. Motor sport in general – and Formula One in particular – is

primarily a technical challenge. Whoever accepts this challenge and really wants to be of help to this elite force should also know all about this business.

But you are also set tasks – not all of which originate from your department. You are directly answerable to the Board, which may view something in a very different light to how you perceive it from a technical perspective. How do you cope with this split?
MT: Motor sport is predominantly a technical task, but that is not its sole nature. Alongside it is the business side, the public relations work and many other aspects. However, technical achievements determine success or failure in motor sport, and for this reason technical equipment is indispensable.

In 2004, you will have to manage without your partner, Gerhard Berger. To what extent will assuming his duties further keep you away from the technical side of your assignments?
MT: There are predominantly two areas which have mainly been developed by Gerhard Berger. The first is what we refer to as Business Relations. After the restructuring four years ago, this new department is now established, so I can easily take over this function. The second area concerns public relations work. Gerhard Berger previously undertook two thirds of the work, with the remaining third being dealt with by me. It's already noticeable too – especially on race weekends.

In your case, public relations work in Formula One also entails a certain degree of celebrity. You, Dr Theissen, can be seen every other week on TV screens – whether you like it or not. Every Formula One fan knows Dr Theissen, but not every fan knows Heinz Paschen. Does it bother you, Mr Paschen, or are you quite happy about it?
HP: Completely happy. We all have a function to fulfil. We act on behalf of BMW in Formula One. This requires Mario to represent the company. He represents our work and our interests very well to the outside world. In order to cover our backs and to pursue the continued development of the engine, this is very important to us. If I were in the foreground, this would certainly not be constructive, mainly because the questions I would have to answer in this position would be completely different questions to those that prevail internally.

Mr Paschen, the best ideas came to the great Formula One constructor Colin Chapman when he sat in the bath or scribbled on tablecloths in restaurants. How does the Head of BMW F1 Engine Development generate ideas?
HP: He hasn't got any time to go to a restaurant . . .

. . . but he's got enough time to take a bath . . .?
HP: ... yes, he's got enough time for that. But when you compare today with those days, everything has become a lot more professional. Today, you must integrate yourself a lot more in team thinking. That is an ongoing process that occurs here. Thoughts do not evolve in the bath; instead, they evolve by working as a team.

Are the times of flashes of inspiration over?
HP: Present day development is a continuous process. It is an evolution from day to day. And if you look back over a year, you will see the work you have done. It is extremely important to recognise this. It is not a single idea that leads to success, but rather the subsequent implementation of complex projects. The ingenuity of earlier times may have worked, but nowadays teamwork is what is required.

How can one best represent your collaboration at the interface between motorsport manager and engine maker?
MT: We work next door to one another, and our doors are usually open. It is a constant balancing act. Subjects like engine concepts, phases of development, production and use of engines come from Heinz. Decisions are taken jointly. I provide the framework, the strategy, the partnership with Williams, the resources provided to us by the company, the incorporation of BMW Motorsport into BMW and the external contacts mentioned previously.

Your English partners, Sir Frank Williams and Patrick Head, eat lunch together every day. Do you do the same?
MT: We still do that, on top of all the rest. We mainly go to the BMW canteen together.

Mr Paschen, when was the last time you said: "No, Dr Theissen, I would have made a different decision"?
HP: We have always been in agreement about every new engine – right from the very start and taking into account the opinions of our experts in the team. For example, regarding what the cylinder head should look like. We were all very much agreed on this. You also need harmony in such matters, especially if you want to make decisions regarding such conceptional basic developments. Once the product has been completed, you cannot discuss strategic decisions. These have to be sorted out at the outset with regard to the long term. Our casual and informal method of cooperation naturally gives us a huge advantage in this respect.

Mr Paschen, the 2003 season is now history. When did you and your colleagues start turning your thoughts towards 2004?
HP: Our initial thoughts evolve very early on. We started work on the concepts in January, and then began construction work at the end of February. In between we halted work because of the discussed changes to the regulations, which delayed the concept phase somewhat. Despite this, we still succeeded in getting the engine for 2004 onto the test bench in July – sooner than we managed in 2003.

A three-litre engine, distributed over ten cylinders – the standard values in the regulations have existed for years and still only permit the smallest of increases. How do you manage to make your team continuously perform to its best ability and bring about success in a sport where every gram and every incremental increase in horsepower counts?
HP: It is an enormous challenge. For an engineer, development will never stop. It always carries on. New things are always being added. Admittedly, if the regulations remain the same, the degree of difference will certainly change. However, the challenge facing the engineers continues to be that of further development. And that is the motivating factor.

But if an engineer is increasingly limited by regulations which become stricter from year to year, how can he still go to work with enthusiasm and drive?
MT: That isn't the situation with us. We orient ourselves according to the regulations…

… Exactly. And because the regulations don't change, year after year the engineers get closer to an objective limit.

MT: Certainly. But what you said about the objective limit is also a point of interest. The physics don't change, but with every new idea the boundaries of what is technically possible are pushed one step further back. Incidentally, engineers are relatively insensitive to such opinions. This means that so long as a perspective and ideas are present, motivation leading to further development will also exist.

What is the prevailing factor in light of the new regulations: The challenge of a new task – namely developing a high-performance engine with double the previous race performance – or the disappointment at having to forfeit maximum output, and therefore sensational displays, in favour of durability?
MT: As I said, engineers are relatively insensitive in that respect. The new challenge of doubling the race performance is just as great as achieving the highest number of revolutions per minute or obtaining a new peak performance value. As far as that goes, it is a task which is just as difficult, just as demanding and just as interesting.

Can costs actually be saved in that way? And to what extent are we talking about?

MT: Firstly we develop the engine, whereby clearly no costs can be saved. On the contrary, the development becomes more resource intensive because we not only have to design the engine to ensure doubled race performance – we also have to test it. This means that the scope of the tests increases in the development stage. The use of the engine becomes more cost efficient simply because we are building fewer engines. Component costs form the bulk of an engine manufacturer's budget. If we reduce the number of engines, those costs are reduced proportionally. A saving effect can be presumed where total costs are concerned – yet just how much this saving will be still cannot be assessed.

A race performance of 800 kilometres instead of 400 kilometres – for someone who normally drives 20,000 kilometres a year, this seems unimportant. What is the significance of this change for Paschen, the engine builder?

HP: You must work even more precisely on the details. Specialists are being stretched to the limits. We must examine each component individually and see where more money needs to be spent. What change is brought about in the bearing reactions and the acceleration of pistons or valves? Can we expect the engine to withstand these stresses over its required service life? And that's when we decide whether it's acceptable or not. Of course, the safety of components is always determined at the manufacturing stage and in testing. However, the principle remains the same: Whether it be 400 or 800 kilometres, the procedure is the same. Once the objective has been defined, the best solution is systematically developed – in essence, the work is determined by the engineers.

Dr Theissen, this year there was widespread coverage in the media as to whether and how your contract with partner WilliamsF1 should be extended. It was extended to 2009 and incorporates intensified technical collaboration. Apart from the BMW engine, what can we expect the 2004 car, named the FW26, to be like?
MT: Even before the new partnership has finally been agreed, we are optimistic that it will be signed and herald a considerably closer cooperation where development is concerned – particularly in the field of electronics and gearboxes. BMW is already making a significant contribution to the gearbox on the FW26. Furthermore, we are in the process of supporting Williams in other fields such as aerodynamics. It is a question of making the expertise, resources and facilities which BMW possesses as a large automobile manufacturer available to Williams.

Broadly speaking, how should such an intensified technical collaboration between a small English specialist and a German automobile group be viewed?
MT: Project management, above anything else, is crucial for the interaction. We come from different backgrounds. In 1997 when the contract was completed, BMW and Williams were two companies that had no dealings with each other. One company is from the highly specialised area of Formula One with the appropriate experience. Small, quick and responsive, focused on this sole task. We, BMW, are an automobile manufacturer with a wide array of technical expertise and resources that a Formula One team can never have. This mainly includes the skills of our engineers in the Research and Innovation Centre (FIZ), as well as the computers, simulation processes and testing facilities available there. If we want to link the special strengths of both partners, it is only possible to do so using joint project management.

So there are employees who constantly think about how these two threads can be optimally interwoven?
MT: They don't constantly think about it – that sounds amorphous. It's a clearly defined and structured procedure. Project management is a question of jointly considering what we want to do, which projects we want to start and who can make which contribution. The project teams are then composed correspondingly, the resources are agreed upon and the timescale is determined – then we're off! The challenge for us lies in combining what were originally two independent units in such a way that we ultimately pack more punch than a pure Formula One team.

**The fact that we are gathered here today is also a sign that technology transfer in Formula One is most easily achieved by way of personnel headhunting.
The former Head of BMW F1 Engine Development now works for a competitor, one who has shown ample interest in making other new contacts as well. Is it at all possible to protect yourself, and if so, what is the best method?**
MT: In Formula One, what is knowledge one day is old hat by the following day. It helps the competition, but it isn't sufficient to give them the edge. That's why we concentrate on our own strengths. We have deliberately expanded our team from the inside out. Employees from BMW played a decisive role in doing so. There are also many employees recruited directly from university and to whom we gave practical training within the team. We are systematically training our own up-and-coming talent. This results in a high level of identification amongst employees – not just in Formula One, but also with our Formula One team and with BMW. Our own experience tells us that a good team spirit and, of course, a high level of motivation to achieve success together is the best formula against brain-drain.

After the first four years in elite racing, which challenge is in retrospect greater: To come into a new sport and

be competitive from the outset, or trying afresh every year to set the pace? Put another way – a huge premiere or continued peak performance?

HP: A successful start is always a "succès d'estime". But in the long term, continuity is important, at least for an engineer. You have to think several years ahead. It is not just a single idea or a single engine that takes us forwards; it really is the continued progression of team and technology. Success in Formula One demands stamina.

MT: If you had asked me four years ago, then I would have said that the entry into Formula One provided the thrill. Back then we still undertook a lot of improvisation. The structure of the team was not complete. We just completed the engine in time for the first race. We suffered a great deal of damage and sometimes went to the race weekend with the last remaining engines. As far as tension is concerned, it was unbeatable. Today, things look different. We are established as a team, we are familiar with the processes and you can almost speak of a controlled course of action. Now it is naturally a question of reconciling this acquired precision with an undiminished innovative capacity. In other words, we are not allowed to become irresponsible, nor must we always remain on familiar territory. Instead, we must launch a controlled offensive. Permanently. I cannot foresee that it will be an easier task than our entry into Formula One.

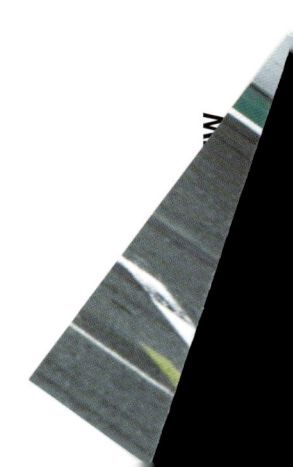

12
WILLIAMS F1
Mobil
Allianz
BR
PETROBRAS
Castrol
hp
Allianz

Results

1. **Ralf Schumacher**
2. **Juan Pablo Montoya**
3. Michael Schumacher
4. Kimi Räikkönen
5. David Coulthard
6. Mark Webber
7. Rubens Barrichello
8. Olivier Panis

GP France

DE FRANCE
MAGNY - COURS 2003

Formula 1

Start: Both BMW WilliamsF1 Team drivers succeed in maintaining their leading positions. Ralf Schumacher leaves pole position to immediately take the lead, whilst Juan Pablo Montoya – his neighbour in the first row – follows him into the first corner. Michael Schumacher does not manage to get off to as good a start. Kimi Räikkönen immediately pushes him out of third place.

Lap 1: Just about to complete his first lap, Rubens Barrichello's car spins – he drops from eighth into last place.

Lap 4: Ralf Schumacher already has a 3.3-second lead ahead of his team mate Montoya.

Lap 10: There is no change in the line-up at the head of the race: Ralf Schumacher leads ahead of Montoya, Räikkönen, Michael Schumacher, David Coulthard, Jarno Trulli, Fernando Alonso and Mark Webber. At the tail end of the race, only Barrichello has provided any overtaking manoeuvres worth mentioning. He is now in 14th position ahead of Nick Heidfeld, Jos Verstappen, Heinz-Harald Frentzen, Giancarlo Fisichella, Ralph Firman and Justin Wilson.

Lap 15: Coulthard is the first of the leading pack to come into the pits. He falls from fifth to ninth place.

Lap 16: Räikkönen, Trulli, Firman and Frentzen ensure that the pits are a flurry of activity.

Lap 17: Montoya and Michael Schumacher enter the pits at the same time. The lifting jack has to be fitted to the Colombian's car a second time – his pit stop takes almost three seconds longer than that of the reigning World Champion.

Lap 18: Ralf Schumacher is the last of the leading pack to come into the pits. Lasting just 6.4 seconds, his pit stop time is the best among the elite drivers. Together with the lead he has already opened up, this ensures that he can maintain his lead ahead of Montoya.

Lap 30: The line-up at the head of the race remains unchanged. Ralf Schumacher has managed to extend his lead ahead of his team mate to 8.1 seconds, whilst Montoya has placed an 8.7-second gap between himself and Räikkönen. They are followed by Coulthard, who is ahead of Michael Schumacher, Trulli, Alonso, Webber and Olivier Panis.

Lap 36: For those drivers racing with a three-stop strategy, the second stop phase does not bring about any change in the line-up.

Lap 40: Montoya starts to close the gap between himself and his team mate.

Lap 45/46: Within the space of two laps, both Renaults are forced out of the race due to technical problems.

Lap 49: With Räikkönen having made his third refuelling stop in the previous lap, his team mate Coulthard now comes into the pits. There is a problem with the refuelling rig during the Scot's pit stop – the spare rig has to be used instead. After a 17.4-second stop, Coulthard drives off impatiently, dragging his refueller to the ground.

Lap 51: Race leader Ralf Schumacher and Montoya, who is trailing him by almost three seconds, catch up with the tail end of the field. Montoya decides to make an early pit stop.

Lap 52: Ralf Schumacher also makes his third pit stop ahead of schedule. He resumes the race after 7.6 seconds, entering the circuit just ahead of his team mate.

Lap 53: Michael Schumacher is the last of the leading pack to refuel. Following his pit stop, the World Champion is in third place ahead of Räikkönen and Coulthard.

Lap 54: Over the following laps, Ralf Schumacher is able to extend his lead ahead of Montoya from 1.2 seconds to over 14 seconds. There is no more overtaking.

Lap 70: Ralf Schumacher wins his second Grand Prix in eight days. With team mate Montoya taking second place on the podium, this victory is the second one-two finish in succession for the BMW WilliamsF1 Team.

From 0 to 100 km/h

The initial races did not bode well. All the more reason to be satisfied with the latest successes.

A victory in Monte Carlo, two podium positions in Montreal, a one-two-victory at the Nürburgring and another at Magny-Cours! What a transformation – the FW25 going from problem child to paragon in the space of a few races. BMW WilliamsF1 Team driver Juan Pablo Montoya outline the two extremities of performance with complete recognition: "I cannot remember a team ever turning a situation around in such a way. When you think back to how we began the season . . ."

The start of the season did in fact leave much to be desired. The results of the initial races of the season made for sobering reading. No victories, no pole positions and only 35 World Championship points from the first six races. In comparison, the team's main rivals, -Ferrari and McLaren-Mercedes, notched up 64 and 63 points respectively within the same period of time.

The question was being asked, each time increasingly critically,: why? The Team consistently stood by its opinion that the FW25 had great potential, as Ralf Schumacher repeatedly confirmed: "The new car definitely has great potential. It is, however, extremely new and we must first understand it correctly in order to be able to really exploit its potential." Ralf Schumacher was right: the WilliamsF1 BMW FW25 is not an evolutionary development upon last year's model. The superiority of Ferrari during the previous season forced the BMW Williams F1 Team into developing a wholly new model with a completely new interaction between the tyres, chassis, aerodynamics and axle load distribution with a considerably reduced wheel base. BMW Motorsport Director Dr Mario Theissen commented: "When the concept is driven forward the opportunities are greater than when the concept is merely evolved – but the risk involved is also greater. This risk can mean that the car may be good in principle, but it may be difficult to use it's full potential from the beginning, and it may simply require time to master." Despite the complexity of the task, Ralf Schumacher made a prediction with impressive accuracy whilst in Malaysia: "In four to five races' time, we will be able to win races." Although the prediction was accurate, hardly anyone believed the adopted Austrian. At the Austrian Grand Prix, Chief Operations Engineer at WilliamsF1, Sam Michael, confessed: "We only understand 75 per cent of the car." That was to change. Only two weeks later in Monaco, the FW25 claimed its first victory. Many explained the transformation as a result of the new tyres developed by partner firm Michelin, which paired magnificently with the characteristics of the WilliamsF1 BMW FW25. It was an important step, yet not the only one, as Patrick Head emphasises: "Even if Michelin did provide us with outstanding material, it wasn't down to the tyres alone."

Describing exactly what the crucial stages of development were is, of course, a difficult task for any Formula One team. Yet in addition to the BMW engine, probably the most powerful engine within elite racing, racing success at distinctly different circuits such as Monaco, Canada, Nürburgring and Magny-Cours demonstrates that the entire package was also greatly developed with regard to mechanical and aerodynamic efficiency. "The fact that we are now winning at circuits which increasingly depend on aerodynamics and the right car set-up is immensely satisfying", says Theissen, heaping praise on partner WilliamsF1 midway through the season: "I have rarely seen such an improvement during a season, and therefore congratulations to WilliamsF1."
The BMW Motorsport Director refers particularly to the progress in the area of aerodynamics and car set-up: "The wind tunnel was running at full power, and WilliamsF1 had modifications ready for every race. In the middle of the season, great improvements have been made in terms of the car set-up. In addition, our supplier Michelin provided us with the right tyres, which turned out to be superior on dry tracks."
Ralf Schumacher confirms the improvements: "The many times where we have performed well can essentially be attributed to three aspects. Firstly, to the front wings, secondly to the combination of the chimney with micro-wings and thirdly to an obvious detail: the rear fin."
The effects of these modifications on driving are also described by Ralf Schumacher: "The modified front wings have increased the downforce at the front of the car, meaning that the car now handles considerably more smoothly on the front axle and is thus better under braking. With regard to the combination of the chimney with micro-wings, the diversion of hot air from the engine is of utmost importance. Hot air must be diverted in such a way that the aerodynamic flow is not disturbed. This was optimised over the course of the season. The rear fin wasn't simply an addition by WilliamsF1 to increase the surface area available for sponsors; instead, this fin provides stability and increased downforce when changing direction."
All in all, the initial ugly duckling that was the WilliamsF1 BMW FW25 has developed into a beautiful swan within a very short period of time. This achievement is best acknowledged in the words of Juan Pablo Montoya: "The way in which the BMW WilliamsF1 Team improved the car over the course of the season has really impressed me."

BMW

Results

1. Rubens Barrichello
2. **Juan Pablo Montoya**
3. Kimi Räikkönen
4. Michael Schumacher
5. David Coulthard
6. Jarno Trulli
7. Cristiano da Matta
8. Jenson Button

GP Great Britain

Start: Rubens Barrichello is unable to translate his pole position start into leadership of the race. He is forced into third place by Jarno Trulli and Kimi Räikkönen. Ralf and Michael Schumacher hold on to fourth and fifth places respectively.

Lap 1: On the Hangar Straight, Michael Schumacher is attacked by Fernando Alonso, who got off to a great start. Michael Schumacher veers to the right and forces Alonso into the grass. Juan Pablo Montoya uses the opportunity to pass Alonso.

Lap 3: Trulli is able to break away easily. Behind him, the line-up remains as follows: Räikkönen, Barrichello, Ralf and Michael Schumacher.

Lap 6: Part of David Coulthard's McLaren-Mercedes cockpit casing comes loose and flies onto the track. The race marshals react to the debris on the track by deploying the safety car. Cristiano da Matta, Coulthard, Olivier Panis and Ralph Firman bring forward their first refuelling stops.

Lap 8: The race gets underway again.

Lap 11: Barrichello forces Räikkönen out of second place.

Lap 12: An evidently mentally deranged protester runs across the racetrack. He is overpowered by track security personnel and led away. The race marshals again deploy the safety car. Fourteen drivers, including the first ten, use this stage to make their first refuelling stop. Behind the safety car, the two Toyotas are suddenly in the lead, with Coulthard in third place.

Lap 16: Second restart. Da Matta leads ahead of Panis, Coulthard, Trulli and Räikkönen. The Finn immediately climbs two places. In 12th, 13th and 14th place are Montoya, Alonso and Michael Schumacher. All three lost a considerable amount of time during the initial refuelling stop since they could only be serviced after their teammates.

Lap 17: Räikkönen overtakes Panis. Barrichello forces Ralf Schumacher out of sixth place.

Lap 18: Ralf Schumacher is overtaken by his teammate.
Lap 20: Ralf Schumacher is forced to make an unscheduled pit stop: A blocked water cooler, caused by parts from a broken spoiler, is causing the water temperature to rise rapidly. After removing the foreign body, he re-enters the race in last place. For the remainder of the race – and for the first time this season – Ralf Schumacher will not occupy any of the points-winning positions.
Lap 24: Michael Schumacher briefly leaves the track during his duel with Jenson Button for 13th position.
Lap 31: Da Matta has to make a pit stop, allowing Räikkönen to take the lead. At the same time, Panis is overtaken by Barrichello, meaning that the Frenchman is now in fifth place.
Lap 32: After battling it out for several laps, Michael Schumacher succeeds in forcing Jacques Villeneuve from ninth place.
Lap 35: Räikkönen makes a pit stop. Barrichello now leads ahead of Montoya and Alonso. Räikkönen re-enters the race behind the Spaniard and just ahead of da Matta.
Lap 39: Montoya and Alonso make a pit stop.
Lap 40: Barrichello is in the pits. Räikkönen leads.
Lap 42: For the second time in this race, Barrichello overtakes Räikkönen. This time he forces him to make a driving error and takes the lead.
Lap 48: Michael Schumacher is able to pass Trulli to take fourth place. Räikkönen makes another driving error and is forced out of second place by Montoya.
Lap 51: Coulthard overtakes da Matta to take sixth place.
Lap 59: In the penultimate lap, Coulthard forces his way past Trulli into fifth place.
Lap 60: Barrichello secures his sixth Formula One victory, winning ahead of Montoya and Räikkönen.

The dolphin dives

McLaren-Mercedes promised a revolution from their new MP4-18A.
However, the fans and competitors are never likely to see just how good the great white hope is.

The announcement from McLaren boss Ron Dennis at the start of this year was clear: "We know for sure that simply improving the MP4-17D will not be sufficient. What we are striving for is an out-and-out quantum leap with the MP4-18A."
Even Ron Dennis' second announcement was equally as frank: "The new car will only be put into use when it is clearly better than its predecessor and having achieved the same level of reliability."
The McLaren patriarch made a third observation: "Launching a new car in the middle of the season is immensely difficult due to the logistics involved. Consequently, we will only adopt the MP4-17D when we are truly certain that the new car is 100 per cent fit for racing."

Within the mesh of these statements hid one of the most confusing stories that ever existed about a new model in elite racing. It is a story which threw up more questions than it answered, week after week. Is the new McLaren-Mercedes really as good as expected? How are the tests coming along? When will it be put into action? Will it ever be put into action?
Only one thing was clear – something that had been successfully attempted by competitor Ferrari in the previous season: The new McLaren would only be introduced during the course of the season. The background to this decision could be seen in the performance of the previous model which, after initial starting difficulties, became better and better over the course of the season. After extensive updat-

ing of the MP4-17 over the winter, it has only really reached its peak performance this season. The backdrop to this development can be understood: Given the complexity of today's Formula One cars, an increasingly extensive trial and testing phase must be allocated in addition to the design and production phase in order to measure the theoretical potential in practice. This takes time, and extends well into the current season if necessary.

The new car, quickly christened "the dolphin" by the media due to its elegant cage-work front design, was first tested in mid-May. At first sight, the obvious characteristics of the McLaren-Mercedes bearer of hope were an extremely narrow and deeply drawn down "nose", very short side housing which had dramatically been drawn downwards at the rear, and a fin which extended far down situated at the centre of the engine covering.

However, it also became apparent that the new technology entailed an array of durability and reliability issues which pushed the race deployment of the new car further and further into the future. At the beginning of the year, the launch of the car was planned for the Spanish Grand Prix. As the season progressed, the launch was set for the European Grand Prix at the Nürburgring, then for "the second half of the season", and finally for the Great British Grand Prix, when "the dolphin" was meant to surface for the first time.

Two more problem areas further contributed to making the "MP4-18A affair" more difficult to resolve. On the one hand, the MP4-18A fell short of the crash test requirements prescribed by the FIA several times, with the side impact tests in particular creating worry. On the other hand, the practical trials suffered at least two setbacks as Alexander Wurz and Kimi Räikkönen both had severe accidents in the new car. To top it all off, the car was further burdened with an array of technical difficulties. The narrow rear of the car took its toll from a thermal aspect.

From this point on, the MP4-18A project ran the risk of being at the media's mercy. When the thought was first aired in McLaren circles of not launching the car during the current season, nor in the next year – another car has long been planned for 2004 – people quickly talked of the "$ 50 million flop". It is a statement which seemed to be as grandiose as it was inappropriate, as McLaren's Managing Director Martin Whitmarsh was quick to underline: "It looks as if an awful lot of money has been squandered on the 18A. In actual fact, many components and a lot of knowledge went into the present car and into the planning for the future model." This moment did not provide an opportunity for McLaren's competitors to delight in the team's misfortune. One thing was certain: With or without the technology from "the dolphin", Räikkönen's "old" car proved itself fighting fit in the battle for the title – right up to the final race in Suzuka. Ultimately, that is the only thing that matters...

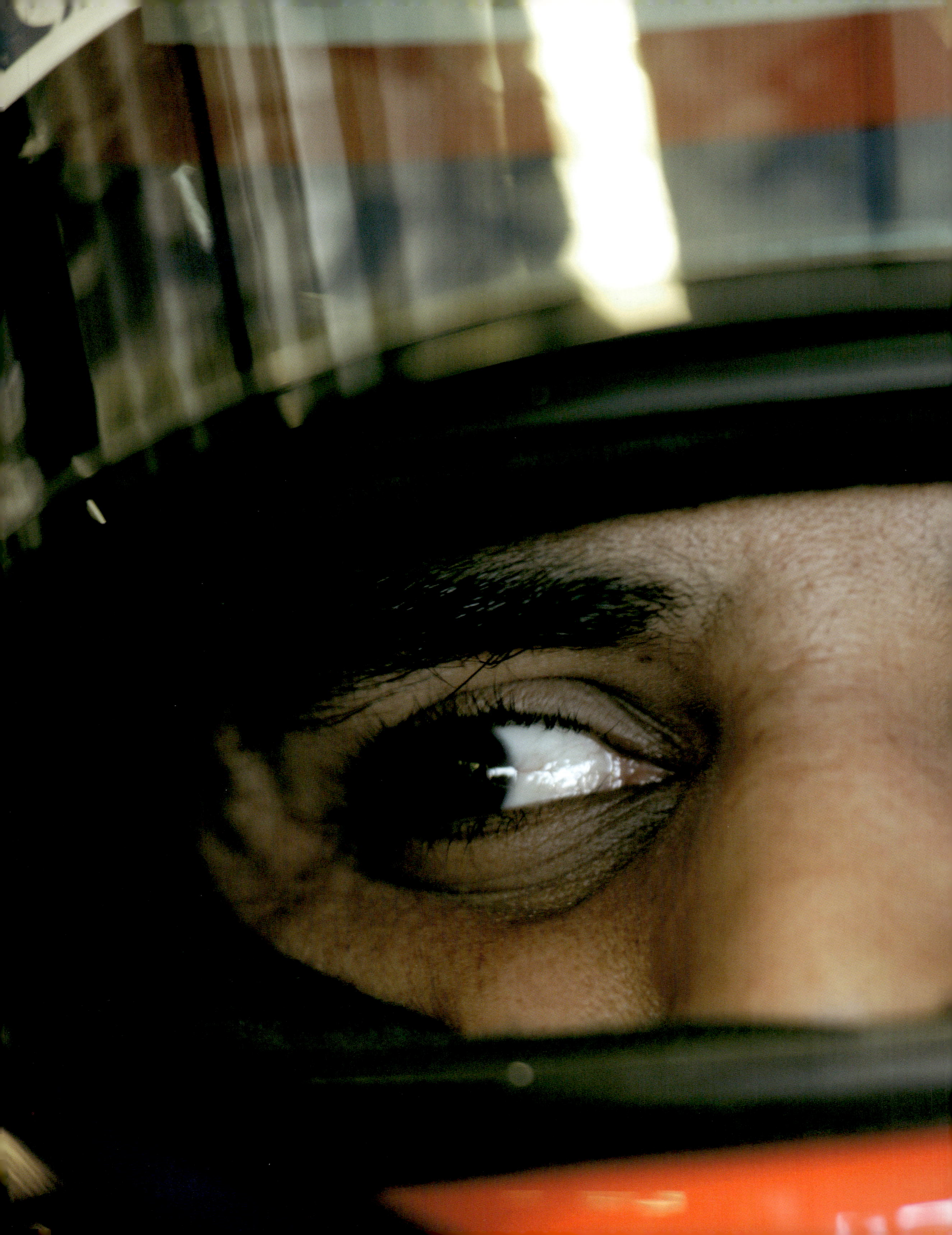

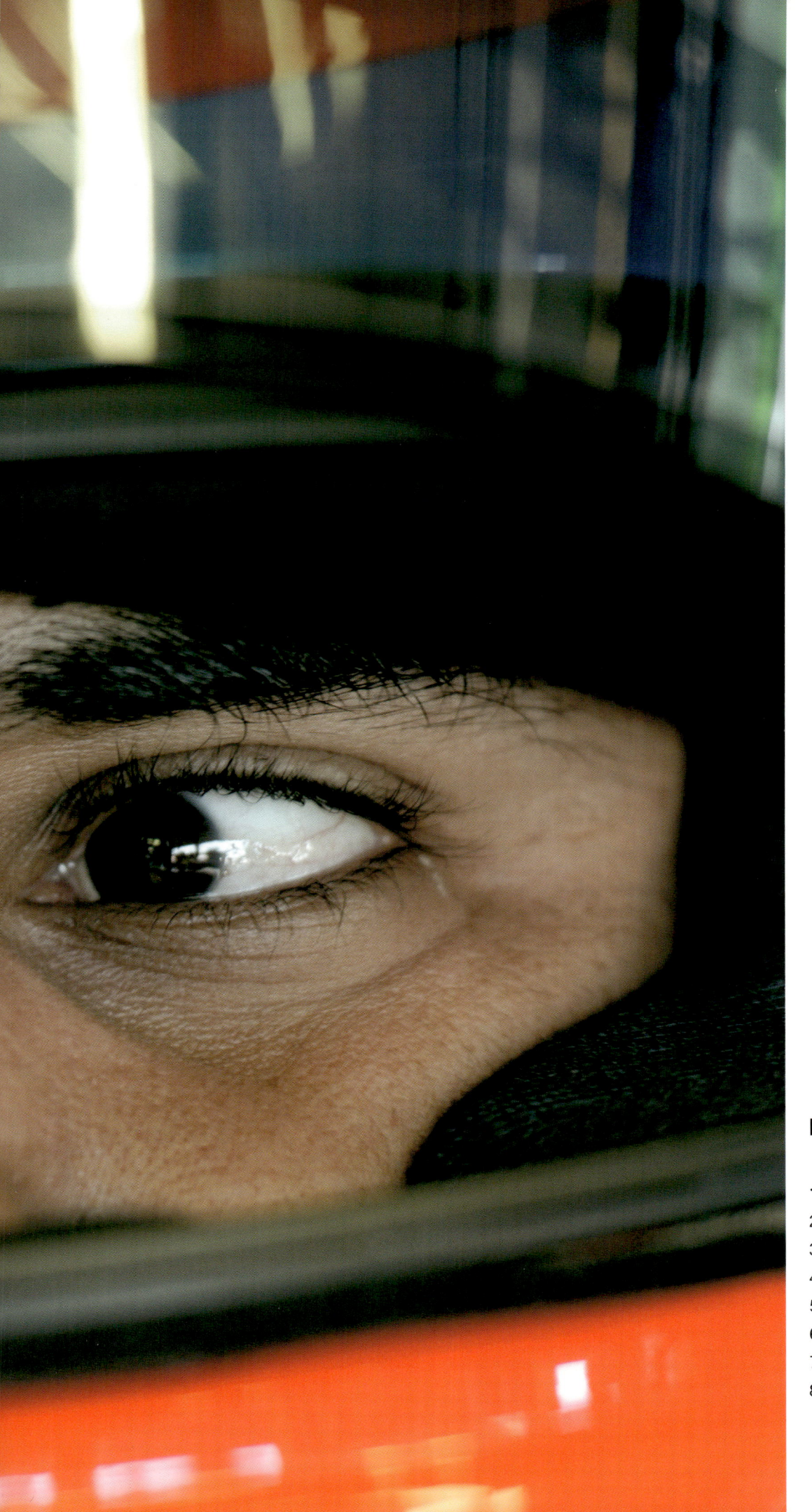

Results

1. **Juan Pablo Montoya**
2. David Coulthard
3. Jarno Trulli
4. Fernando Alonso
5. Olivier Panis
6. Cristiano da Matta
7. Michael Schumacher
8. Jenson Button

GP Germany

Start: Juan Pablo Montoya is able to translate his pole position start into leadership of the race. Behind him, however, there is a certain amount of friction. Ralf Schumacher and Rubens Barrichello, starting from second and third place on the grid respectively, take a while to get going. This is in complete contrast to Kimi Räikkönen, who immediately draws level with Barrichello after starting from fifth place on the grid. Whilst Ralf Schumacher veers to the left to find his line for the first corner, Barrichello sees that he is being squeezed out by Ralf Schumacher and Räikkönen. The three cars clip each other, with Räikkönen being worst affected after skidding at high speed sideways on into the tyre wall. Barrichello is also immediately forced out of the race, whilst Ralf Schumacher manages to reach the pits – where he quits the race, too. The starting accident has repercussions for those further back in the starting line-up. Ralph Firman slides into the rear of Heinz-Harald Frentzen's Sauber, which then clips Justin Wilson, who in turn causes Jacques Villeneuve's BAR to spin. The race marshals decide to deploy the safety car.

Lap 1: Behind the safety car, the leading eight cars are as follows: Montoya, Jarno Trulli, Fernando Alonso, Michael Schumacher, Mark Webber, David Coulthard, Olivier Panis and Cristiano da Matta.

Lap 4: The race gets underway once more.

Lap 7: Montoya is already able to put 2.3 seconds between him and the two Renault drivers; Coulthard forces Webber out of fifth position.

Lap 14: Trulli prompts the first round of refuelling stops, giving Montoya an 8.8-second lead ahead of Alonso and Michael Schumacher.

Lap 17: Montoya and Michael Schumacher enter the pits at the same time. The difference in their refuelling times reveals distinct strategies: Montoya has a three-stop strategy, whilst Michael Schumacher has a two-stop strategy. The race leader is now Alonso, who will make his refuelling stop one lap later.

Lap 21: After the majority of the initial refuelling stops are over, Montoya has a lead of approximately 16 seconds over Trulli, Alonso and Michael Schumacher.

Lap 31: Michael Schumacher succeeds in overtaking Alonso as he veers slightly off the track at the beginning of the circuit.

Lap 33: Meanwhile, Montoya's lead has grown to such an extent that he is able to complete his second pit stop without losing first position.

Lap 38: Trulli and Michael Schumacher, in second and third place respectively, enter the pits at the same time. Their positions remain unchanged.

Lap 43: Owing to a markedly late second pit stop, Coulthard is able to push past Trulli and take fourth place.

Lap 50: Leading by almost one minute, Montoya makes his third pit stop. Da Matta also makes a pit stop, thereby once again losing sixth place to his team mate, Panis, who had refuelled during the previous lap.

Lap 59: Michael Schumacher forces past Trulli on the outside of the kick turn. Unaffected by this, Montoya leads by 53 seconds.

Lap 60: Trulli, who is having problems with his rear tyres, is also overtaken by Coulthard.

Lap 63: Michael Schumacher's rear left tyre is losing air. He has to complete almost an entire lap with the deflated tyre before he can return to the pits. Overall, the Ferrari driver loses over 60 seconds and falls five places.

Lap 67: With a lead in excess of one minute, Montoya wins the race. Coulthard and Trulli take second and third place. Behind Alonso, the two Toyota drivers, Panis and da Matta, also qualify for winners' points. The remaining points positions go to Michael Schumacher and Jenson Button.

The television court is in session

**A completely normal racing accident? Or an avoidable collision?
What happens when extensive data analysis reverses a decision.**

The race has barely started when the first ruling has already been made. Immediately after the start, a serious chain reaction is triggered on the approach to the first bend. Having started from completely different places on the starting grid, Ralf Schumacher, Rubens Barrichello and Kimi Räikkönen rapidly approach the first braking point almost neck and neck. This formation flight results in a spectacular accident, spelling the end of the race for the three drivers involved.

Whilst the safety car brings an air of calm to the German Grand Prix, the pace is gathering behind the scenes. A quarter of an hour has not even passed since the crash when Race Director Charlie Whiting recommends that the race commissioners penalise Ralf Schumacher. The three commissioners, Nazir Hoosein, Radovan Novak and Waltraud Wünsch make a decision accordingly: "The driver of car number 4 (Ralf Schumacher) caused an avoidable collision in accordance with Article 53 of the 2003 FIA Formula One Sporting Regulations." The penalty awarded for the incident: At the next Grand Prix, Ralf Schumacher will be relegated ten places on the starting grid.

Such a ruling comes as a hard blow for Ralf Schumacher – who said it was a completely normal starting accident – and his battle for the drivers' title, as well as for the BMW

WilliamsF1 Team and its fight to win the Constructors' Championship. WilliamsF1 decides to appeal against the ruling. And indeed it does: In the run-up to the Hungarian Grand Prix, Ralf Schumacher's relegation towards the rear of the starting line-up is changed into a fine. The decision to do so was made in Paris during the first ever sitting of the international Court of Appeal of the FIA to be broadcast on television.

An essential, decision-reversing moment came when special remote metering data from all those involved in the accident could be analysed. This data allowed factors such as the time of braking and steering wheel deflection of the three drivers to be examined. This evidence now allowed the FIA Court to consider Ralf Schumacher as not having sole responsibility for the accident.

Such a revision could, of course, call into question the judgement of the three track commissioners. However, they did not have time to reflect – they had to form an opinion immediately after the race. Their ruling was only based on video footage and witness statements taken from those involved – no influential remote metering data and no personal racing experience could be taken into consideration. It is for this reason that such data was increasingly requested in previous years, as the former Formula One racing driver and current television commentator Marc Surer comments immediately after the Hockenheim race: "I am certain that the track commissioners make their judgements to the best of their knowledge and ability. But they only drive cars in road traffic, and not in races. Professional drivers must therefore take their place – preferably former drivers, whose racing careers have only recently come to an end."

This is something that a former racing driver such as Surer wishes to point out: "When a car can accelerate from 0–100 km/h in five seconds, the limits of the conceivable have been reached in the mind of 'Mr Average'. When a car can accelerate from 0–200 km/h in the same five seconds, it destroys all common conceptions. When you have 20 cars accelerating from 0–200 km/h in this five-second period, and every driver in these cars wants to be the first through the first bend, you have to be a professional racing driver to understand what such moments are about."

Because this is the case, the former Formula One racing driver Hans-Joachim Stuck goes one step further and suggests appointing "active racing drivers as track commissioners – preferably the test drivers".

It is an idea which seems reasonable only at first consideration – a belief supported by Surer: "Active test drivers are hardly recommendable for the job. They would be too biased. Take the following scenario: If Heinz-Harald Frentzen ended his career, he would be predestined for the job. Ten years' experience of Formula One – all of which are still recent. The important thing is for the professional to still have the cockpit perspective in his head."

This perspective, as well as being aware that extreme circumstances prevail on the racetrack, is what counts. Surer remarks: "If Ralf's penalty had been upheld in Paris, it would have only meant one thing for me, namely that road traffic rules would prevail in Formula One with immediate effect."

Up, up and away!

London, Milan, Paris, Munich – six Grand Prix circuits have their own particular starting point there.

Airfield racing – that is a word for racing fans of a long gone era. For aficionados of the good old days, the words still ring in their ears: Zeltweg, Siegerland, and of course Silverstone.

The basic idea was obvious: Where passenger jets or wide-bodied transport aircraft have sufficient space for take-off and landing, narrow monopostos and agile sports cars would have sufficient space to trigger their rpm limiter. And they were right, too: In post-war Europe, there were more pressing building needs than the construction of permanent racing tracks. This meant that a converted airfield was a good and cost-effective alternative. A few dozen red pylons, a tractor load of hay bails and several hundred meters of adhesive tape, and it was ready – the racing track for the weekend. This is inconceivable for modern-day racing, but even Formula One races took place under these conditions then. In 1964, heroes such as Jim Clark, Graham Hill and Joakim Bonnier fought it out on the uneven, concrete surface of Zeltweg military airport in Styria. How times have changed. The elite of the racing world, with safety standards unmatched anywhere in the world, today prefers permanent tracks. Formula One racing has no business on an airfield.

Naturally this only applies to racing. Modern-day Formula One is a World Championship. Europe and Australia, Asia, North and South America – elite motor racing is a true global player, dependent on the most modern and rapid methods of transport. It is therefore all too apparent why Formula One would choose to convene at an airport – even if the days of airfield racing are long gone: The airlift Grand Prix.

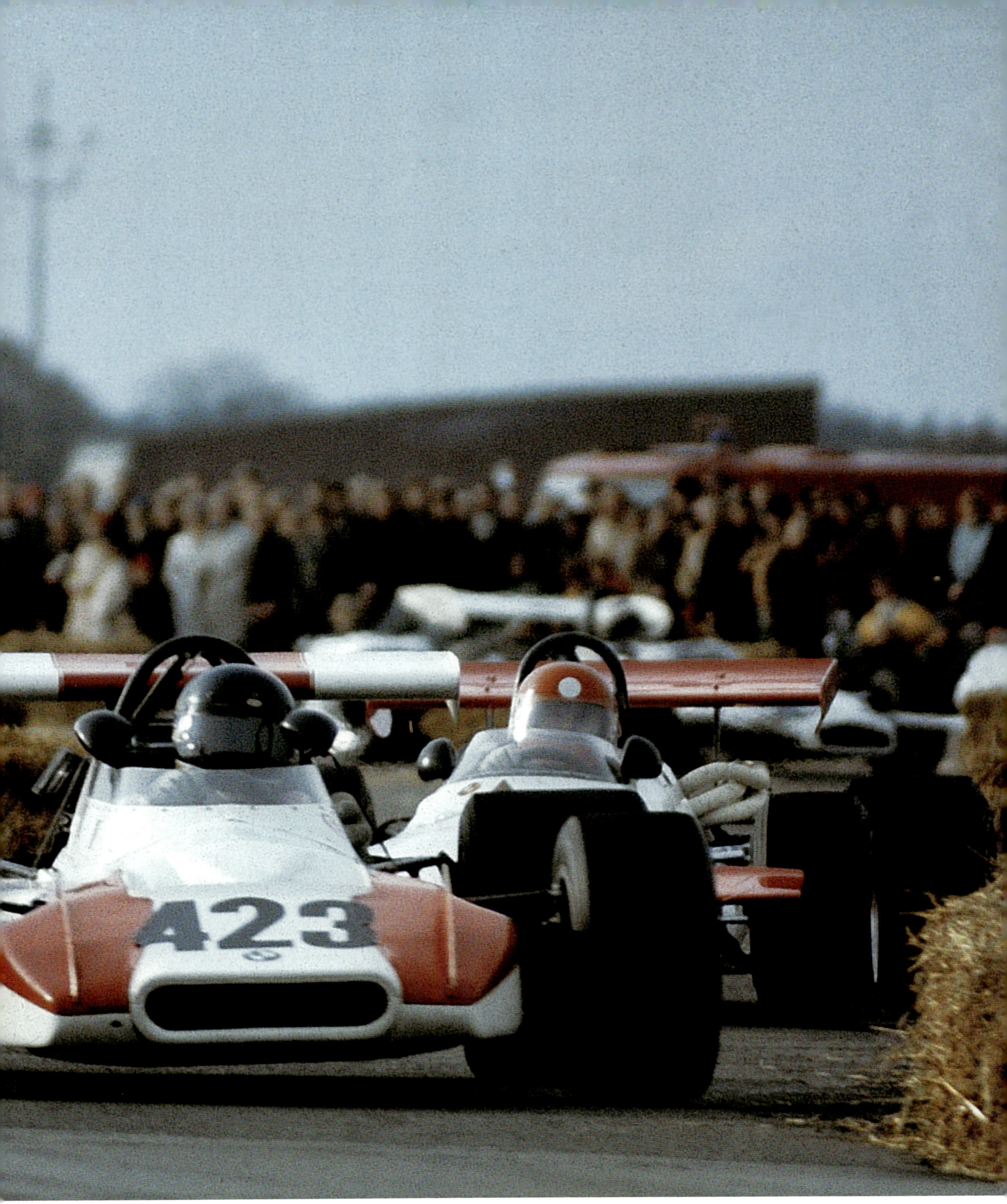
423

There are six dates on the current Formula One calendar when the Grand Prix racing cars must leave their usual racing transporter berths in order to take their place in an aircraft to be taken overseas. At the beginning of the season, these are Melbourne, Kuala Lumpur and São Paulo. Mid-season takes the teams to Montreal, and at the end of the season to Indianapolis and Suzuka.

In keeping with the general image of the elite motor racing world, these trips are organised in accordance with a meticulous procedure, not least because Bernie Ecclestone's "FOM" (Formula One Management) is responsible for the transportation. For each overseas trip, the British company sends four chartered Boeing 747s on the long journey. After all, the top teams take around 25 tonnes of hi-tech material with them to each race.

The jumbo jets take off from London, Milan, Paris and, more recently, from Munich. FOM allocates to each team a binding window of time, during which the equipment must be brought out onto the apron in a form suitable for transportation, i.e. in containers and on palettes. BMW partner WilliamsF1 transports its possessions from London, whilst the airport in Paris is responsible for around six tonnes of BMW's equipment bearing the white and blue BMW logo. Regarding the logo, at BMW – just as at WilliamsF1 – importance is attached to a well-maintained corporate identity, even on the airport apron. The aluminium containers are like the tarpaulin sheets pulled over the palettes containing the Formula One cars. They are in identical team colours as are the lorries which drive to the circuits for the European Grand Prix. Order is imperative.

For each racing weekend – and the same is true of an overseas Grand Prix – BMW has ten new engines in tow. If everything goes well, four of them will be used – an engine each for the Friday and Saturday morning, and an engine each for final training/qualifying on Saturday and the race on Sunday. These four engines are immediately sent back to Munich after the race, and the required replacement engines are dispatched for the next overseas race.

Yet sometimes, as in the experience of Peter Schoob, who is responsible for overseas transport at BMW, it is not entire engines, but rather only certain individual parts which must be taken from airport to airport and then brought quickly to the track in time for the race. Remembering the 2001 season, the trained air freight forwarding agent says: "In Malaysia we needed a new fuel pump really quickly."

Those that travel frequently know about the problems associated with travelling. "We would prefer to dispatch smaller parts not travelling with the FOM charter directly from Munich. Yet if the flight is routed via certain airports, caution is advised. London is problematic, as is Paris. They are huge airports where the chance of luggage being lost during unloading is simply too great." There are two ways of ensuring that airfield racing in its literal sense does not finish in the pit lane.

The first alternative is to deliver urgent freight directly to Paris or London using one's own forwarding agents. Doing so at least eliminates the danger of the transported goods being mistakenly overlooked when being transferred from one plane onto another. If taking a risk is completely out of the question, as was the case involving the pump for Kuala Lumpur, plan B is invoked: "In such a situation, one of our forwarding agents will put the part in the carry-on luggage and personally bring it to the location." The cost of doing so is best left unsaid.

In order to try and maintain at least some control over costs, the overseas Grands Prix are held together at the start and at the end of the season. Instead of flying to each location separately, there are around-the-world tickets. Paul Singlehurst from WilliamsF1 says: "At the beginning of the season we were on the move from 16 February until early April. Part of the team and all of the materials that belonged to them went from London to Melbourne, and from there directly to the next race in Kuala Lumpur and subsequently to São Paulo. If we had returned to base after each race, these expenses would have doubled or tripled."

Inside **BMW**

119

Yet even so, this three-stop journey – in which 1 kg costs $38 to transport – carrying a total weight of 24,660 kg costs almost $937,000. A further four tonnes are transported by ship.
Australia, Malaysia and Brazil are also combined into one phase of the season, just as the US and Japan are at the end of the season. Only the Canadian Grand Prix stands in isolation to the rest of the races. Yet wherever the equipment is sent, there remains the fear that not everything will arrive as it should. The word "damaged goods" hangs like the sword of Damocles over every shipment, even more so when the goods in question include hi-tech Formula One equipment. In Munich, however, the reaction is calm: "Up until now we have never had a problem. The only exception to this was when an entire shipment arrived one day later than planned. At our inaugural Grand Prix in Australia in 2000 of all places, the jumbo jet had engine damage and had to make a stop in Amsterdam." It was this very same

airport which played a role one year later in Formula One's operation "Big Lift". After the events of September 11 and prior to the Grand Prix in the USA in Indianapolis, security had been stepped up to the highest level. Every container had to be checked in Europe for explosives, and only Amsterdam airport had a facility which was large enough to screen the aluminium containers.

It was a precautionary measure which has thankfully been avoided in subsequent years. Instead, people have been able to concentrate on a normal season finale. The trip to Indianapolis and Suzuka places special demands on logistics, for which BMW does not wish to rely on Ecclestone's FOM. Instead, the entire team takes responsibility for the shipment. "When packing the equipment up at the airport, it should be ensured that the necessary crates of beer for the closing party have not been forgotten. That's one mistake that could not be rectified at the circuit! After all, what we're talking about here is original Bavarian wheat beer…"

Marlboro
A DOHÁNYZÁS SÚLYOSAN KÁROSÍTJA AZ ÖN ÉS KÖRNYEZETE EGÉSZSÉGÉT!
CHAMPAGNE
MUMM
vodafone
SIEMENS

GP Hungary

Results

1. Fernando Alonso
2. Kimi Räikkönen
3. **Juan Pablo Montoya**
4. **Ralf Schumacher**
5. David Coulthard
6. Mark Webber
7. Jarno Trulli
8. Michael Schumacher

Start: Fernando Alonso translates his pole position start into leadership of the race. Ralf Schumacher and Juan Pablo Montoya, starting from the dirty side of the track in second and fourth place respectively, get off to a bad start. Mark Webber, Rubens Barrichello, Kimi Räikkönen, Jarno Trulli, David Coulthard and Michael Schumacher reach the first bend before the two BMW WilliamsF1 Team drivers.

Lap 1: Ralf Schumacher battles with his brother and Montoya for seventh position. In doing so, he spins and drops back to 18th position.

Lap 2: Alonso already has a three-second lead ahead of Webber, who is under pressure from Barrichello. Ralf Schumacher overtakes Zsolt Baumgartner and Jenson Button.

Lap 3: Alonso extends his lead to 7.3 seconds. It is clear that second-placed Webber is holding up the other pursuers. When attacking the Australian, Barrichello misses the chicane – costing him two places.

Lap 6: After overtaking Heinz-Harald Frentzen, Jos Verstappen and Giancarlo Fisichella, Ralf Schumacher is now pushing Olivier Panis from twelfth place. Alonso is leading 14 seconds ahead of Webber, Räikkönen, Trulli, Barrichello, Coulthard, Michael Schumacher and Montoya.

Lap 9: Ralf Schumacher overtakes Justin Wilson and moves into eleventh position.

Lap 11: Jacques Villeneuve loses tenth position to Ralf Schumacher.

Lap 13: The two leaders, Alonso and Webber, enter the pits and Räikkönen takes over the lead.

Lap 15: Räikkönen and Trulli are now refuelling; Alonso resumes the lead once again. Ralf Schumacher pushes Nick Heidfeld from seventh place.

Lap 17: One lap after Barrichello and Montoya, the two Schumacher brothers make their refuelling stop.

Lap 20: Räikkönen is the winner of the first round of refuelling stops; he has managed to advance ahead of Webber into second place. Fifth-placed Barrichello has a serious accident. At the end of the finishing straight, his left rear wheel sheers off together with the suspension. The Brazilian hits the tyre barrier hard, but remains uninjured. Over the course of the lap, Ralf Schumacher is able to progress into seventh place ahead of Coulthard.

Lap 30: Meanwhile, Alonso's lead has grown to such an extent that he retains the lead despite making his second refuelling stop. Ralf Schumacher pushes his brother out of sixth position.

Lap 39: Michael Schumacher, the last of the drivers with a three-stop strategy – the exceptions being Coulthard and Button – makes his refuelling stop. He drops down into eighth place. Alonso is leading ahead of Räikkönen, Coulthard, Montoya, Webber, Ralf Schumacher and Trulli.

Lap 43: Coulthard makes his last stop and is able to slip back into the race ahead of Michael Schumacher.

Lap 46: Ralf Schumacher overtakes Webber and takes fourth place.

Lap 48: Frentzen runs out of fuel and is stranded.

Lap 49: Alonso initiates the third round of refuelling stops.

Lap 54: After all refuelling stops have been completed, Alonso leads by 24 seconds ahead of Räikkönen. Montoya is ten seconds behind the Finn, whilst Ralf Schumacher is in fourth place, Coulthard in fifth.

Lap 62: Montoya spins, but is just able to maintain third place ahead of Ralf Schumacher.

Lap 70: Alonso wins his first Grand Prix – the first Spaniard to do so and the youngest winner in the history of Formula One.

Alonso, the youngest...

You could call him a whizz kid – one which is continually being brought back down to earth by his manager.

At the time of the Hungarian Grand Prix, he was 22 years and 26 days old. After 1 hour 39 minutes and almost one and a half seconds, Fernando Alonso is one of the youngest Formula One champions in history. "It's like a dream. I'm afraid of waking up."

There are several chapters to Alonso's dream: At the beginning of May when the 21-year-old shot down "La Castellana" in central Madrid in his Renault R23 as part of a promotional event, 75.000 enthusiastic fans lined his way. At the Spanish Grand Prix, the Circuit de Catalunya was covered by a sea of blue and yellow flags. Not the blue and yellow colours of his Renault team, but the blue and yellow colours of his Asturian home town of Oviedo. By the time of the Hungarian Grand Prix, one thing is certain: The Spaniard Fernando Alonso has established himself within the small group of elite racing drivers. He has done so without having the privilege of a rare place in one of the cars belonging to the three teams, which in the past seven years have won all the titles and claimed almost all the Grand Prix victories. The opinion leading English trade magazine "Autosport" celebrates Alonso as "the most exciting new thing of the season", and ranks the Spaniard alongside the likes of Juan Pablo Montoya and Kimi Räikkönen. On the other hand, Alonso's manager and team boss, Flavio Briatore, is unmoved by such statements. He knows only too well that things work differently in Formula One: "At present, it is still too early to say if he'll be the next Michael Schumacher. What we can say at this stage is that Fernando learns tremendously fast." And he has to – otherwise he would not hold the attribute that has accompanied him for years: Alonso, the youngest… He won the much sought after Formula Nissan title at 17, followed by his first Formula 3000 race just under a year later. When he entered Formula One in 2001, he was not old enough to hire a car in many countries.

For Alonso's entry into Formula One, manager Briatore relied on his tried-and-tested preliminary training model: He placed his pupil with Minardi, as he had done with Giancarlo Fisichella and Jarno Trulli before him. This is the place to learn the basics of Formula One at a leisurely pace and without the huge pressure to see results.

Whilst most observers had celebrated newcomer Räikkönen as being the huge discovery of the season that year, other insiders had long since directed their excitement towards Alonso. The performance given over and over again by the Spaniard in the Minardi profoundly impressed them: Very fast, consistent and cleverly raced.

This was sufficient reason for Briatore to once again take the pressure out of the system. He removed his pupil from elite racing for a year so that he could sample the hard life of a Renault test driver. Fernando did so without complaint. At the start of the 2003 season, he confirmed to his manager: "Regardless of how difficult it was to be unable to take part in the races, my year as a test driver has ultimately achieved more than all the years prior to it put together. Today, I am a better racing driver." Fresh from his stint as a test driver, he delivered results as Renault's permanent driver: Seventh at the opening race in Australia, third in Malaysia, third in Brazil, sixth in San Marino and then a sensational second place in front of his home crowd in Spain – only beaten by five-times World Champion Michael Schumacher.

It was only in Brazil that the Spaniard made a mistake in his selection of technique, but he showed extreme determination with regard to this error when he intentionally ignored the yellow flag that was being waved. The only reason this was not punished by the race marshals was because he drove at full speed into the wreckage and thereby punished himself. Alonso's excuse was more than flimsy: "I was careful, I didn't think that there would be so much wreckage." You suddenly realise just how young Alonso still is. When he entered Formula One in 2001 – a move which surprised many people – he was the third-youngest Grand Prix entrant in history. The only two people to make their Grand Prix debut at a younger age than Alonso were the New Zealander Mike Thackwell and the Mexican Ricardo Rodriguez. In Malaysia, Alonso was the youngest person ever to start from pole position, which even had his rough-and-ready manager in raptures: "He is a natural talent." Even after his first ever victory in Hungary, Alonso remains modest: "I don't think that I have made it into the history books of Formula One just yet. To do that, I still have to achieve an awful lot." When asked, Alonso reveals his understanding of "achievement": "Becoming the youngest Formula One World Champion, for example."

Background GP Hungary

Budweiser
KING OF BEERS
BR
PETROBRAS
Allianz
BMW
NiQuitin CQ
hp

Results

1. Michael Schumacher
2. **Juan Pablo Montoya**
3. Rubens Barrichello
4. Kimi Räikkönen
5. **Marc Gené**
6. Jacques Villeneuve
7. Mark Webber
8. Fernando Alonso

GP Italy

Start: Michael Schumacher emerges as the winner from the initial duel against Juan Pablo Montoya. Jarno Trulli is the third driver to enter the first bend. The champion of the Hungarian Grand Prix, Fernando Alonso, starts from the last position on the grid and collides with Jos Verstappen. Both drivers are forced into the pits.

Lap 1: Montoya makes a determined attack against Michael Schumacher in the second chicane. The Ferrari driver is only just able to defend himself against the attack. Trulli, who in turn is attacking Montoya, drops out of the race due to a hydraulic failure.

Lap 3: Michael Schumacher has a 1.2-second lead over Montoya. They are followed by Rubens Barrichello, Kimi Räikkönen, David Coulthard, Marc Gené (standing in for a shaken Ralf Schumacher), Olivier Panis and Jacques Villeneuve.

Lap 4: Just before the "Parabolica" corner, the rear left tyre on Cristiano da Matta's Toyota bursts whilst travelling at around 340 km/h. Da Matta spins out of the race.

Lap 11: Coulthard is the first to begin the refuelling stops.

Lap 13: Räikkönen and Gené make their pit stops.

Lap 15: With 4.9 seconds separating him and Montoya, Michael Schumacher enters the pits. Montoya is able to stay out on the track one lap longer, thus taking the lead.

Lap 16: After his pit stop – lasting 8.4 seconds – Montoya re-enters the race in second place 3.4 seconds behind Michael Schumacher. They are followed by Barrichello, Räikkönen, Coulthard, Gené, Villeneuve and Panis.

Lap 19: Montoya begins to catch up with Michael Schumacher.

Lap 24: For the first time, the gap between the two leading drivers is less than two seconds.

Lap 29: With a considerably better set of tyres than beforehand, Montoya is only 0.9 seconds behind the Ferrari driver.

Lap 32: Montoya has to make his second pit stop. After 9.0 seconds, he is in fourth position behind Gené. Coulthard also makes a refuelling stop and falls back into sixth place behind Barrichello, who made his pit stop during the previous lap.

Lap 34: Michael Schumacher's second pit stop lasts 9.2 seconds. He re-enters the race just behind Gené.

Lap 35: Gené enters the pits. Michael Schumacher is now leading, with a 1.6-second gap separating him and Montoya.

Lap 37: Owing to brake problems, Panis ends his race in the pits.

Lap 39: The two leaders have almost identical lap times.

Lap 40: Michael Schumacher and Montoya catch up with Heinz-Harald Frentzen. Whilst the Sauber driver immediately lets Michael Schumacher through, Montoya slips a further 1.1 seconds behind the Ferrari when lapping Frentzen. After direct contact has been lost, Montoya secures his second place.

Lap 45: Fifth-placed Coulthard coasts to a standstill.

Lap 51: Seventh-placed Frentzen drops out of the race due to gearbox problems. This allows team mate Nick Heidfeld, now in eighth position, to qualify for a potential place in the winners' points table.

Lap 53: Michael Schumacher wins the Italian Grand Prix – it is his 50th victory for Ferrari. Montoya comes in second ahead of Barrichello, Räikkönen, Gené, Villeneuve and Mark Webber. Alonso takes eighth position after overtaking Heidfeld on the last lap.

The substitute

The after-effects of concussion: the grand appearance of the substitute driver, Marc Gené.

On Thursday, Ralf Schumacher was still cracking jokes. In response to the question of what the doctors had examined following his accident during testing in Monza, he offered an example of his self-deprecation which is so well liked within the drivers' enclosure: "My brain impulses – and surprisingly they found some." A day later, Ralf had lost his sense of humour. On the Friday, after free practice, Ralf felt increasingly unwell and subsequently made a critical error during the qualifying: "I braked too late on the approach to the first chicane, forcing me to drive straight on." The mistake cost the team dearly as the race officials declared the lap time achieved by the BMW WilliamsF1 Team driver to be void. It was a truly dismal situation for Ralf Schumacher's Championship challenge who, with 58 points, lay fourth in the standings behind Michael Schumacher, Juan Pablo Montoya and Kimi Räikkönen and was considered to be a contender for the World Championship title. Things, however, were to get worse. Late on Friday night, Ralf's headaches and nauseousness worsened. So, at 7 o'clock on Saturday morning, Ralf consulted Formula One's doctor, Professor Sid Watkins, who advised Ralf not to race: "Under so much stress, it is entirely feasible that even trained sportsmen would suffer a relapse." Even before the paddock woke up to the usual chaos, Ralf Schumacher and his wife, Cora, were already sat on a plane heading for Salzburg. No race, no fight for victory, all hopes of taking the title were dashed. His disappointment was so great that he did not even want to watch Sunday's race on television.

Equally as understandable as Ralf's frustration was the joy expressed by another member of the BMW WilliamsF1 Team. Immediately after Ralf pulled out of the race, test driver Marc Gené received a phone call which he described as the "best wake up call of my life". At 7.30 a.m. WilliamsF1's Chief Operations Engineer, Sam Michael, told him that he would have to contest the Italian Grand Prix for the BMW WilliamsF1 Team.

This is the dream of every test driver and substitute driver. After clocking up tens of thousands of test kilometres, this is their one chance to showcase their own ability before a global audience, and in this case, in one of the best cars on the starting grid.

It is an opportunity that one can never be certain of, as Gené himself admits: "I signed a contract to be a test driver and substitute driver, but I didn't sign this contract in the hope that I would ever get to race. This race is a true bonus – I never thought that this would happen to me."

Being given an opportunity and actually taking advantage of an opportunity are all too often quite distinct concepts. After receiving the wake up call from Sam Michael, it took Marc Gené over an hour to reach the race track. It did not help that he was staying in a hotel a fair distance away. Furthermore, the usual traffic near a large event such as this and the fact that he did not have a valid permit for the drivers' parking spaces also cost him time. At the very last minute, Gené introduced himself to the race director, Charlie Whiting. From thereon in, however, everything ran according to plan.

The Spaniard felt particularly encouraged: "Juan Pablo helped where it mattered – tips about the circuit, the start, refuelling stops." Gené's objective was clearly divided into compulsory and voluntary tasks. The compulsory task: "To bring in as many points as possible for the team." The voluntary task: "To undertake an authentic race alongside the world's best drivers." Gené was familiar with Monza. In the week before he had completed a Grand Prix distance there during a test session. He had also raced recently in the Nissan World Series. In order to remain fit, he had asked the team management at the start of the season to be allowed to race in a monoposto class as well as undertaking test runs. What was truly new for Gené was the individual time trial in final qualifying and the refuelling stops: "I was more nervous before qualifying than I was before the race."

He need not have been. As the first driver out in the final qualifying session, therefore racing on a slow, rubber-free track, he performed perfectly and managed to secure a respectable fifth place. Crossing the finishing line in fifth place at the end of the race itself confirmed the Spaniard's high level of ability. Even in the ensuing fuss around him, he retained his sense of modesty: "I am extremely satisfied, especially since it was an error-free weekend." That's one way of saying it. It can also be said in the words of Juan Pablo Montoya: "Marc's achievement was amazing. He did an absolutely brilliant job."

The tyre test

They can be the key to victory – or defeat. Likewise, they can mean a hard slog or a lap blessed with good fortune.

Marc knows precisely what is in store for him. It is still early at the Circuit de Catalunya, and there is silence everywhere. No traffic on the entrance road, no spectators in the stands, no press, no crowds of people – neither in the drivers' area nor in the pit lane.

Marc knows that today will be a day of hard graft. Two or three Grand Prix distances are on the schedule for today. And whilst he slips into the BMW WilliamsF1 Team blue and white racing overall, they are long since ready for the race.

Neatly aligned they stand like padded towers, waiting to be put into action, carefully wrapped up in shining blue plastic covers from which cable after cable protrudes. Under the covers, each tower contains an average of 40 kg of black mass surrounding the wheel rim. Handmade from over 200 materials and substances. There's oil in there, and steel too, as well as sulphur compounds and resins, textile fibres and rubber.

All mixed according to secret recipes and formed into tyres, they become the only point of contact between the high-tech racing cars and the asphalt-covered racing track. A wide, black and adhesive link between a team's goals and their achievement.

Today, Marc will take each set of tyres and data will be wrought out of each one. He will listen to them, and each weakness – no matter how small – and each apparent strength will be located, collated and evaluated. He will dissect them.

Marc Gené is qualified to do so. He knows it and his team knows it. And the people at Michelin know it too. Pierre Dupasquier, Head of Sport at Michelin, which has long been the tyre supplier to the BMW WilliamsF1 Team, summarises the Spanish test driver: "Marc is smart. He's got brains. He's calm. Despite very good lap times, he can summon up the necessary calm to perceive everything and collate all relevant observations. Furthermore, he can carry out a highly accurate analysis."

Marc Gené has been a test driver at BMW WilliamsF1 Team for three years. He spends 100 days a year driving circuits of the track, constantly searching for ways to shave off fractions of a second for his team and for his two team mates, Juan Pablo Montoya and Ralf Schumacher. Each season, around 40 of these test days are dedicated exclusively to tyre tests. So much time is needed because tyre testing is a science, testing the limits of chemistry and physics. Laboratory analyses at 300 km/h.

In spite of everything, "Professor" Gené outlines his working day in a matter-of-fact and concentrated manner. The tool of his trade, a 900-bhp Formula One racing car, may sound like speed, euphoria and adventure, but for Gené its purpose is precision, empirical values and synthesis: "We start early in the morning with around ten sets of tyres lying waiting in the pits. In addition, there is an appropriate number of reference tyres to ensure throughout the day that changes in the track do not go unnoticed. So, we begin by using the reference tyres, then the first set of new tyres, then the reference tyres for comparison, then the second set of new tyres, then back to the reference tyres, and so on and so forth."

Five or six laps are driven with each set of tyres. Over half a day, there is time to perform approximately ten test sessions. Yet before these test drives even get underway, all

Inside **BMW**

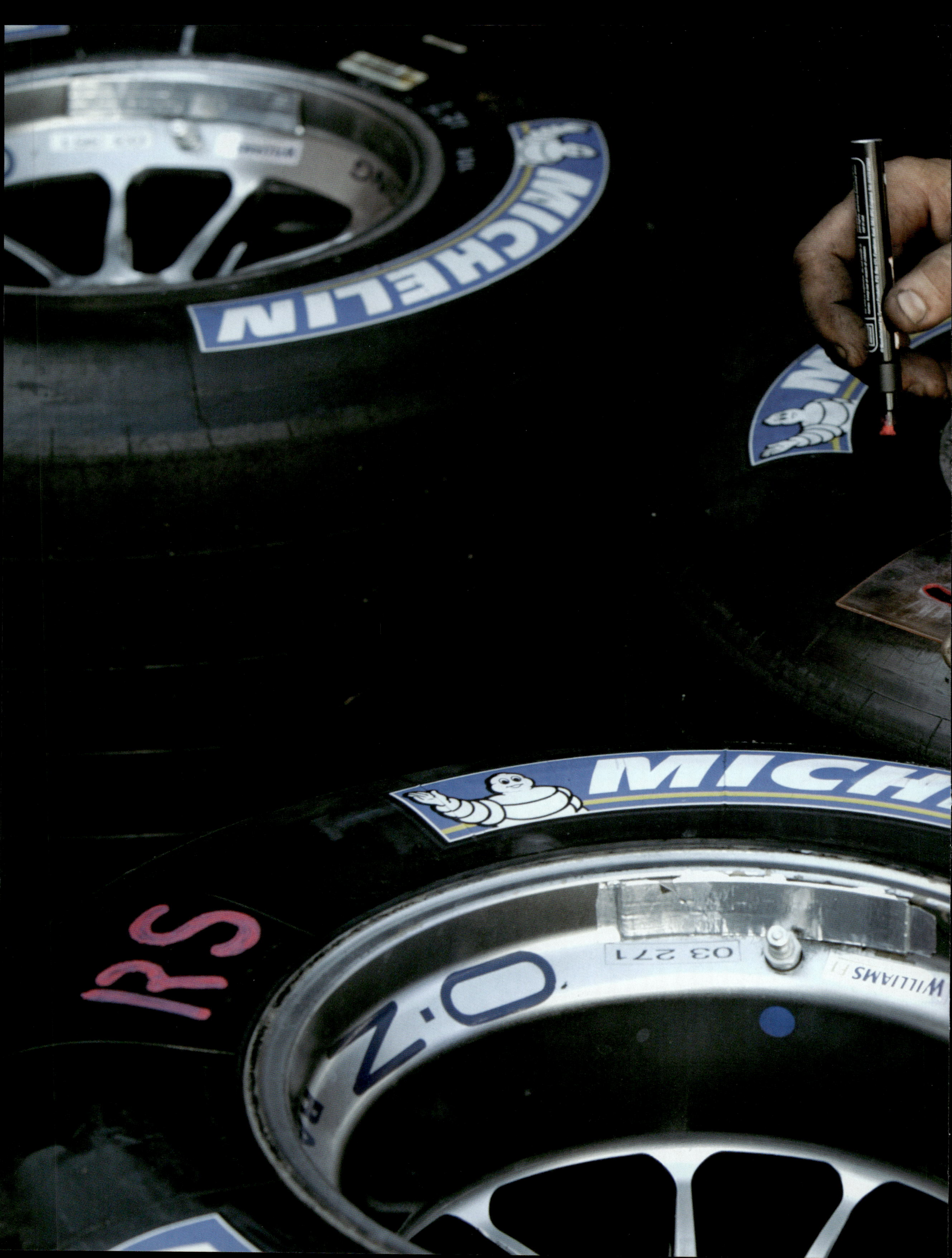
MICHELIN
03 271
WILLIAMS F1

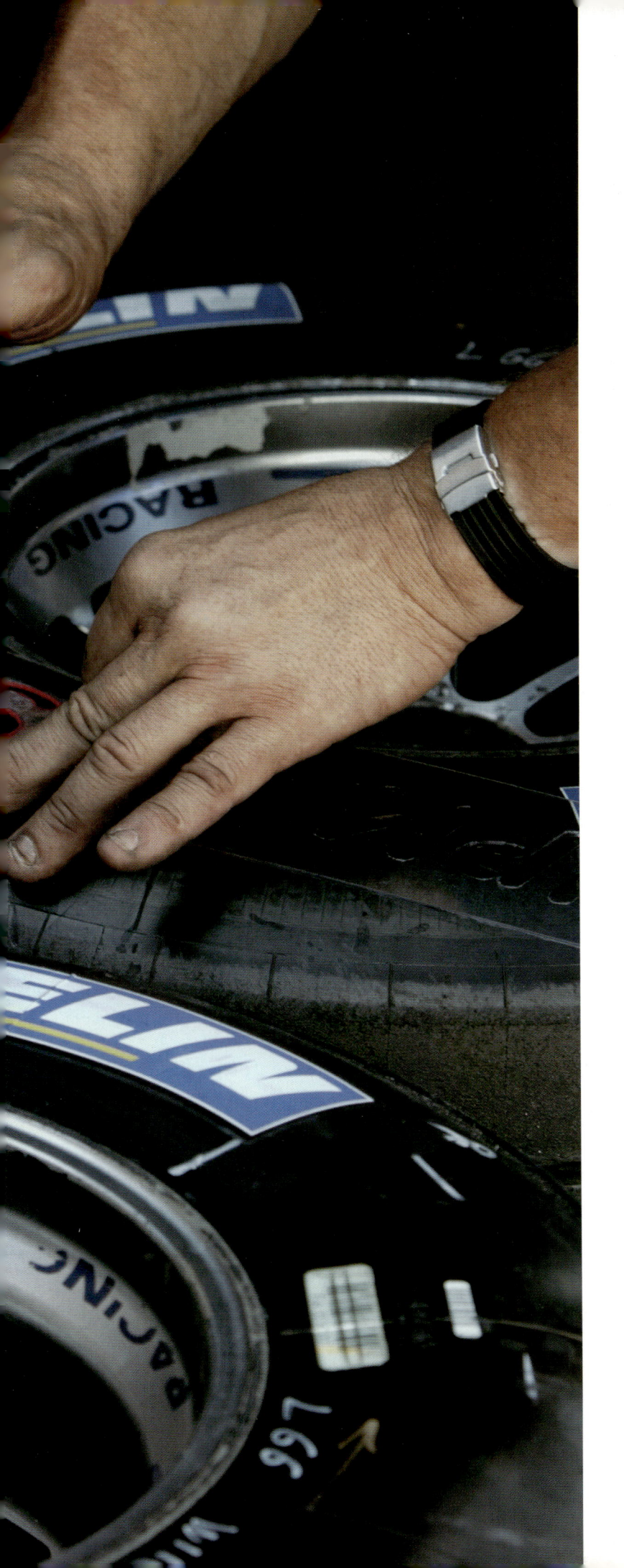

members of the team must be certain that the test car is perfectly tuned. Gené is in a position to know: "An unbalanced car makes no sense at all when performing tyre tests. Therefore the first set of tyres that we use early in the morning are known as set-up tyres. I use these to tune the car, and only when I say that the car is now correctly tuned can we perform the ten tests."

Even if the procedure is always the same, no two tyre tests are ever the same. This maxim presents Gené with completely different tasks: "There are two types of tyre testing days. One is used to work on the tyre composition, whilst another concentrates on the tyre construction."

The hidden meaning of this is explained by Dupasquier from Michelin: "The construction is related to the car, whilst the composition relates to the track."

Given the chance, Gené would concentrate on researching the construction of the tyre: "Where composition is concerned, it is already known that the softer composition is usually the quicker. Softer tyres have better traction and better braking ability. Theory, at least, stipulates this. However, a large question mark looms where construction is concerned. If it makes the car more agile, it results in increased oversteer or whatever else. It's unchartered territory."

In this connection, Gené feels challenged by the fundamental issues: "In relation to the method of constructing a tyre, it is actually a question of fundamentals. It's like deciding if an engine should have eight or ten cylinders. For this reason, it's essential not to be wrong. If you are off the mark in this field, then you are really off the mark. Michelin can quickly change the composition of a tyre, but if there are errors in construction, then it even takes them a while…"

Regardless of whether the composition or construction is being put to the test, the schedule for the afternoon presents the team with a new task. The schedule includes what Gené refers to as long runs: "We select the best three sets of tyres from the morning test session, which we then use to complete 15 to 20 laps of the circuit in the afternoon. In the morning we are looking at what the tyres can do, and then in the afternoon we ensure that they can withstand a long run without any problems."

Overall, a day of testing such as this will easily involve 130 to 150 laps being completed, all of which are performed at the upper limit – something that Michelin Head of Sport Dupasquier insists on: "You have to drive really close to the limit. Not just one fast lap. No – every lap must be a fast lap, otherwise we will learn nothing about our tyres."

Furthermore, such work requires a driver with a truly special profile of requirements: A high level of ability without an overblown ego. This is confirmed by Gené, the racing driver with a university degree: "We must be as fast as the actual racing drivers, but we don't drive in any races. Nor can we allow ourselves to make any mistakes when driving because that completely messes up the schedule. The teams consequently look for highly experienced drivers to use as test drivers. In short, we must be fast, make no mistakes and, when driving, constantly think about what is happening to the car at that moment in time. There are so many drivers who come back to the pits with their pulse racing. When you ask them about their impressions of the test drive, they are silent. They are concentrating so much on driving fast that they are unable to concentrate on the car."

Test drivers must be something special. Tyre testers must be something extra special. Michelin's Head of Sport has his own ideas about this breed of test driver: "Testing tyres is boring. Nobody likes it. Out for three laps, then back in again, then five laps, then 25 – each lap is stoical and executed with the precision of a Swiss watch."

Confronted with this theory, Gené puts up fierce opposition: "No – on the contrary, tyre testing is extremely satisfying. If aerodynamic or mechanical parts are being put to the test, there are few opportunities to come across as a good driver. The times involved in these tests are barely comparable; for non-specialists, they are barely comprehensible. Yet when testing tyres, you know that you are allowed to drive the quickest possible lap time."

Whether testing parts or tyres – there is a sudden and abrupt flash in each and every one of them: They are all born racing drivers. In all their endeavours, they want their lap times to reflect well on themselves. That's easier to do with tyre testing. Or, as Marc Gené puts it, laughing: "Whenever I see tyre testing on my work schedule, I'm happy."

Inside **BMW**

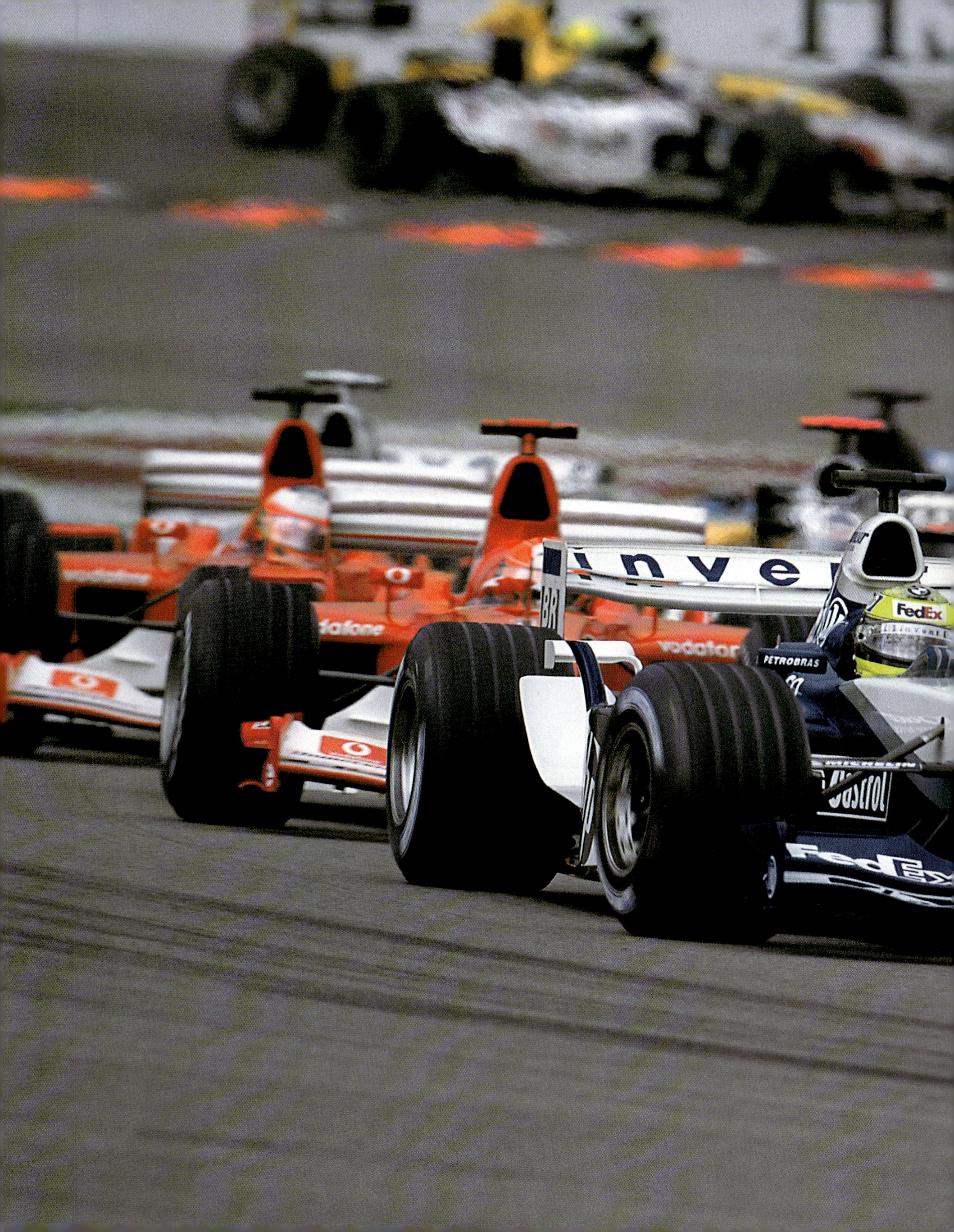
FedEx
PETROBRAS

Results

1. Michael Schumacher
2. Kimi Räikkönen
3. Heinz-Harald Frentzen
4. Jarno Trulli
5. Nick Heidfeld
6. **Juan Pablo Montoya**
6. Giancarlo Fisichella
7. Justin Wilson

GP USA

Start: Starting in pole position, Kimi Räikkönen immediately goes into the lead. His neighbour in the first row, Rubens Barrichello, is overtaken by Olivier Panis, Ralf and Michael Schumacher. Juan Pablo Montoya drops from fourth to seventh position.
Lap 1: Räikkönen has a 1.6-second lead over Panis.
Lap 2: Light rain affects some parts of the course. David Coulthard forces Barrichello out of fifth position.
Lap 3: Ralf Schumacher overtakes Panis. Montoya attempts the same manoeuvre with Barrichello. The two cars clip each other, leaving Barrichello stranded on the gravel. Montoya drops down to eighth position behind the two Renault drivers.
Lap 4: Montoya overtakes Jarno Trulli.
Lap 5: Michael Schumacher passes Panis. Fernando Alonso overtakes Coulthard. The rain gets heavier.
Lap 6: Panis, Jacques Villeneuve and Ralph Firman come into the pits for wet tyres. The rain causes Alonso to make a mistake and he is overtaken by Coulthard and Montoya.
Lap 7: With the rain easing off, Michael Schumacher drops behind Coulthard, Montoya and Alonso into sixth position.
Lap 10: The rain stops. All the drivers who have switched to using wet tyres now require dry tyres again.
Lap 15: Ralf Schumacher's first pit stop. Montoya overtakes Coulthard to take third place.
Lap 17: Montoya and Coulthard enter the pits at the same time. Montoya experiences problems with the refuelling equipment. His pit stop lasts five seconds longer than Coulthard's.
Lap 18: The heavy rain returns. Alonso comes into the pits, but keeps his dry tyres.
Lap 19: Räikkönen comes into the pits – he also keeps his dry tyres. Despite recommendations from his team, Heinz-Harald Frentzen insists on wet tyres. Montoya receives a drive-through penalty because of the incident with Barrichello.

Lap 20: The rain gets heavier and heavier. Despite this, race leader Michael Schumacher is given dry tyres at his second pit stop. Second-placed Trulli is also given dry tyres. Mark Webber takes the lead.

Lap 21: Michael Schumacher rectifies his choice of tyre and changes to wet tyres. Frentzen passes Jenson Button.

Lap 22: Race leader Webber flies off the track. Ralf Schumacher drops out of the race after a spin. Räikkönen and Alonso switch to wet tyres. Coulthard now leads ahead of Frentzen and Button. Montoya – racing with dry tyres – has to complete his penalty in the pit lane. Since it is not permitted to carry out work to the car during the drive-through penalty, the Colombian is forced to complete a further lap on dry tyres despite the chaotic weather situation.

Lap 23: Racing on dry tyres, Coulthard gets into difficulty and drops behind. Button overtakes Frentzen and assumes the lead. Montoya is finally able to change to wet tyres. He is one lap behind.

Lap 28: Button, using Bridgestone tyres, extends his lead to 5.8 seconds. Michael Schumacher pushes Räikkönen out of third place. Montoya overtakes Coulthard.

Lap 29: The rain stops.

Lap 30: Nick Heidfeld passes Justin Wilson and takes sixth position. Coulthard comes into the pits.

Lap 33: Michael Schumacher passes Frentzen.

Lap 35: The Ferrari driver closes the gap between him and Button. Heidfeld pushes Alonso out of fifth position.

Lap 38: Michael Schumacher takes the lead.

Lap 42: Engine failure spells the end of the race for Button. Michael Schumacher leads ahead of Frentzen.

Lap 48: Michael Schumacher makes a refuelling stop; Frentzen leads the race.

Lap 49: Frentzen enters the pits, re-entering the race in third position behind Michael Schumacher and Heidfeld.

Lap 51: Heidfeld makes his last pit stop.

Lap 55: A fast-approaching Räikkönen overtakes Frentzen. Having taken second position, Räikkönen still sees that there is everything to play for in the world championship battle.

Lap 63: Trulli passes Heidfeld and takes fourth place.

Lap 67: Montoya passes Giancarlo Fisichella – and moves into sixth place.

Lap 73: Michael Schumacher wins the race ahead of Räikkönen and Frentzen. Second-placed Räikkönen still has a small chance of winning the title. For Montoya, who finished in sixth position behind Frentzen, Trulli and Heidfeld, the title fight is over.

The hard plight of the men at Sauber

At the Indianapolis race, the Sauber drivers provided the most successful day in the history of the team – despite this, they have both been dismissed.

Ten points in one race! Even the victorious Ferrari ensemble was unable to leave the US Grand Prix with more points to its name. How much must such a result have delighted a team which up until now only lay ahead of Minardi in the world championship table? This makes the reaction of the team boss in Indianapolis all the more amazing. He once again assured the media that his team would definitely feature new drivers for the coming year.

At the start of the season, the Swiss ensemble took to the starting line with a surprising pairing of drivers: Nick Heidfeld and Heinz-Harald Frentzen. Two Germans together in a team, both sharing the same home town of Mönchengladbach. As Heidfeld's manager, Werner Heinz, admits: "It is a rather unusual arrangement, because two drivers from the same country can be problematic for the sponsors. On the other hand, Nick and Heinz-Harald are two outstanding drivers, and that's what should count."

The whole world was now dying to see these "two outstanding drivers". Their initial situation could not have been more distinct, but their objectives could not have been more similar – meaning that the two men from Mönchengladbach would not get on well with one another. One driver, Nick Heidfeld, in the fourth year of his Formula One career that was finally meant to take him over the threshold from being a talented young hopeful to an established star. The other driver, Heinz-Harald Frentzen, approaching the end of his career at 36 years of age – but still recognised as a fast driver and therefore a potential stumbling block on the career path of every young driver. Both of them competing not only on the track, but also off the track for the affection of the public and sponsors. Conflict between the two seemed to be pre-programmed. Instead of the Mönchengladbach City Championship, would it become a battle between team mates?

Things turned out completely differently. Instead of being able to profile themselves as drivers, they were restricted by the technology of the Sauber Team. The Swiss team, which shone in 2001 in fourth place behind the top teams in the constructors' championship, underperformed almost consistently throughout the 2003 season. This led team boss Peter Sauber to take stock early on in the season – to his bitter disappointment: "There are several reasons for our poor performance. Firstly, it must be said that the car's aerodynamics are not good enough. Secondly, the tyre manufacturer Michelin has made enormous progress in comparison to our tyre providers, Bridgestone. This has been of enormous benefit to our competitors for fifth and sixth position, such as Toyota and Jaguar. Thirdly, the reliability of Formula One cars is improving more and more. There are barely any race results in which the elite teams fail to claim all the points. Finally, the Renault Team has established itself as the fourth top team surprisingly clearly."
What is striking is that Sauber fails to mention an important area when listing the problems facing the team.
The Swiss has nothing to criticise about the performance of the two German Formula One drivers. He expressly states: "Our modest performance is down to the car and the tyres – but not the drivers."
In the meantime, the drivers have displayed loyalty to their team. At regular press conferences, they endeavour to avoid any criticism of the car, engine or the tyres. It has been a difficult task for the two drivers, since it became increasingly apparent halfway through the season that Peter Sauber was planning to replace both drivers for the coming season.
Insiders were not at all surprised when, at the end of August, Giancarlo Fisichella was announced as one of the new drivers for 2004. For years now, Sauber has been trying to attract the fast Italian. What is surprising, however, is that the Brazilian Felipe Massa is to be paired with Fisichella. This is the same Massa who was dismissed from Sauber just one year before, and who had clearly been beaten back then by Heidfeld in the training duel alone by 11:5.
The fact that Massa then switched to Ferrari as a test driver and that the Italians retained their option on the Brazilian as a potential successor to Rubens Barrichello has got the sector thinking. Does Sauber wish to pay the important engine supplier Ferrari a favour and allow Massa a further year of learning and assessment? Or has Massa demonstrated previously hidden qualities in his year as a test driver in Maranello?
Both questions are of secondary importance to Heidfeld and Frentzen. They are more worried about their own careers in Formula One.

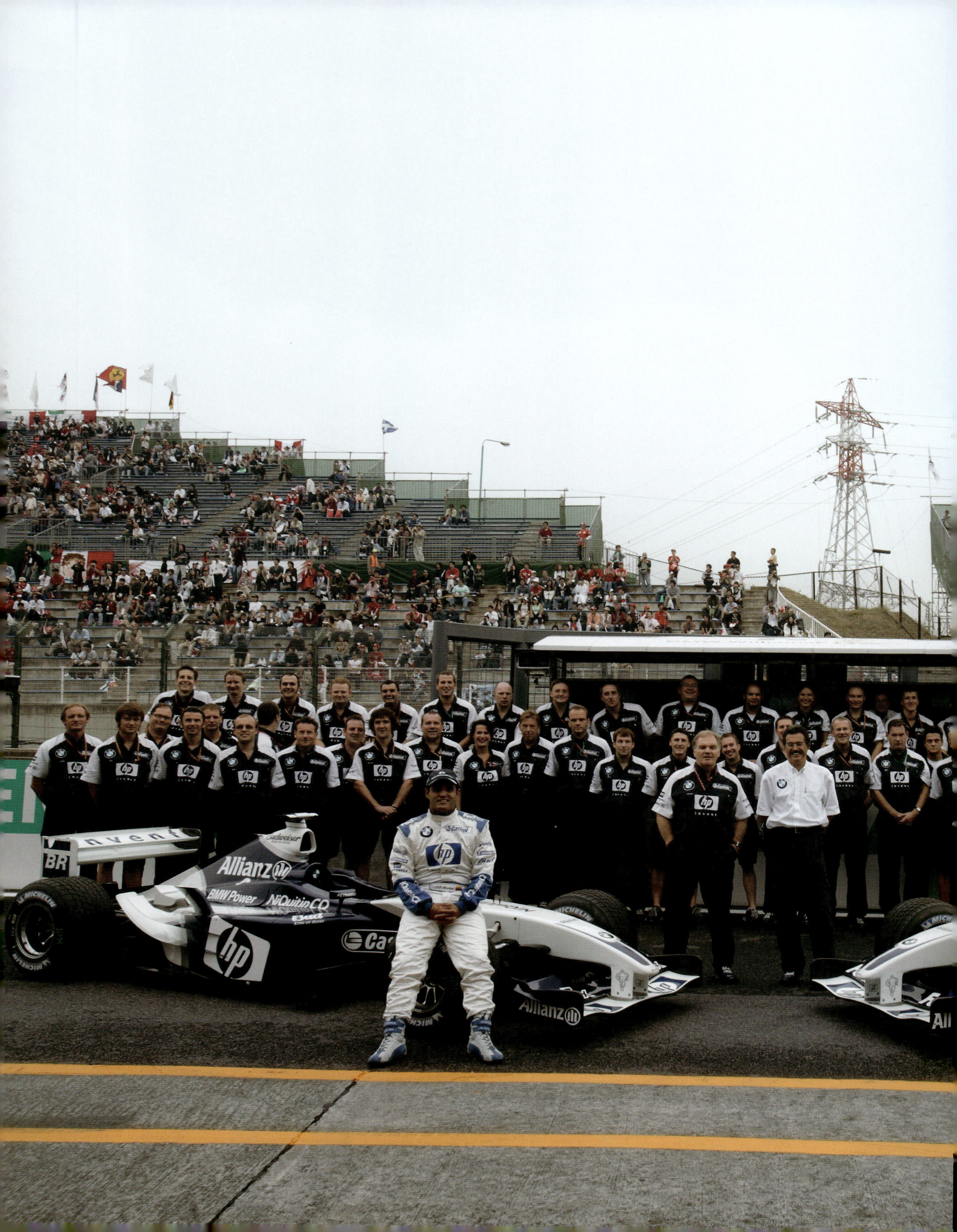
Allianz
BMW Power
NiQuitin CQ
hp
MICHELIN

GP Japan

Results

1. Rubens Barrichello
2. Kimi Räikkönen
3. David Coulthard
4. Jenson Button
5. Jarno Trulli
6. Takuma Sato
7. Cristiano da Matta
8. Michael Schumacher

Start: The start gets underway without a hitch. Rubens Barrichello and Juan Pablo Montoya maintain their positions, whilst behind them Fernando Alonso gets off to such a good start that he is immediately able to overtake the two Toyota drivers starting from the second row, Cristiano da Matta and Olivier Panis.

Lap 1: Montoya overtakes Barrichello in the hairpin bend. One of the World Championship contenders, Kimi Räikkönen, who started from eighth position on the grid, is now sixth. Michael Schumacher has pushed his way up from 14th to 12th position. Jarno Trulli and Ralf Schumacher, who started the race from the last row, have improved their positions to 13 and 14 respectively.

Lap 2: Montoya leads by 3.4 seconds. Ralf Schumacher attacks Trulli, spins and drops back to 19th position.

Lap 3: Montoya extends his lead; Alonso is putting the pressure on Barrichello.

Lap 6: Michael Schumacher attempts to overtake Takuma Sato, who is in ninth place. He destroys his front wing on the rear of the BAR. Following repairs, he is in last position.

Lap 7: Ralf Schumacher overtakes Giancarlo Fisichella to take 15th place.

Lap 9: Montoya, who in the previous lap was still 3.3 seconds ahead of Barrichello, suddenly becomes slower and is forced to allow his pursuer to race past. The Colombian coasts into the pits, where he quits the race due to a hydraulic defect. His team mate, Ralf Schumacher, hits the rear of Heinz-Harald Frentzen's car when trying to overtake him. Ralf Schumacher is able to continue the race, whilst Frentzen is forced into the pits.

Lap 10: Third-placed da Matta sets off the first round of refuelling stops. Räikkönen moves into da Matta's place.

Lap 12: Barrichello, Alonso and David Coulthard enter the pits. This means that Räikkönen is now leading ahead of Jenson Button and Sato.

Lap 16: After Räikkönen and the two BAR drivers have completed their pit stops, Barrichello is once again in the lead. He is followed by Alonso, Coulthard, Räikkönen, da Matta and Button. Ralf Schumacher is in eleventh place after his refuelling stop; his brother Michael is 14th.

Lap 18: Alonso drops out of the race due to engine trouble.

Lap 24: Ralf and Michael Schumacher come into the pits at the same time – their three-stop strategy is now apparent. They rejoin the race in eleventh and twelfth place respectively.

Lap 26: Barrichello and Coulthard – who are also racing with a three-stop strategy – come into the pits to refuel. Barrichello re-enters the track ahead of Räikkönen, Button and Trulli, who are all racing with a two-stop strategy.

Lap 33: After the two-stop drivers (Trulli, Sato, Räikkönen, Button and Nick Heidfeld) have left the pits, Barrichello has a 23-second lead over Coulthard and Räikkönen. He is followed by da Matta, Ralf and Michael Schumacher.

Lap 37: Sixth-placed Michael Schumacher makes his third stop – tenth position.

Lap 38: Da Matta (in fourth place) and Ralf Schumacher (in fifth) enter the pits. With almost identical pit stop times – da Matta on 7.0 seconds and Ralf Schumacher on 7.1 seconds – both drivers re-enter the race in eighth and tenth place respectively. Michael Schumacher separates the two.

Lap 39: Ralf Schumacher wants to overtake his brother. He pulls into his path and thus keeps Ralf behind him.

Lap 40: Barrichello enters the pits. He concedes his lead to Coulthard, but he does manage to re-enter the track ahead of Räikkönen, Button, Trulli and Sato – all of whom are racing with a two-stop strategy.

Lap 41: Coulthard now makes his refuelling stop – Barrichello is once again in the lead. Michael Schumacher miscalculates his braking when attempting to overtake da Matta ahead of the chicane. In doing so, the Ferrari driver comes into the path of Ralf Schumacher, who is also braking harshly, and clips his front wing. Ralf Schumacher is forced into the pits – he re-enters the race in tenth position. The concern amongst the Ferrari team that the incident could have damaged Michael Schumacher's front tyres is proved to be unfounded.

Lap 53: Barrichello wins the final race of the World Championship; Ferrari is the constructors' champion. Team mate Michael Schumacher, finishing in eighth place, secures his sixth World Championship title. Behind Barrichello, Räikkönen and Coulthard also win a place on the podium.

Bad race, good season

The Formula One season does not just comprise Indianapolis or Suzuka. It is 16 races. Viewed together, these 16 races reflect the most successful year for the BMW WilliamsF1 Team.

It is as typically Japanese as sushi and sake. And it is just as much part of the Formula One World Championship finale as the start and finish of the race – karaoke singing in the small log cabins around the legendary Log Cabin Bar in the middle of the Suzuka circuit hotel.
BMW Motorsport Director Dr Mario Theissen and team driver Ralf Schumacher stand there and sing Deep Purple's "Smoke on the Water" and the Beatles classic "Ticket to Ride" at the top of their voices. The Colombian supporters join in the songs, as do Juan Pablo Montoya, his wife Connie and mutual friends. Theissen and the team keep to their word, "After the race, we'll open the beers, one way or another."
One way or another – those seeking sport and competition must take this to heart, this happy but also cruel concept of 'anything is possible'. Involved in this is the whole spectrum of emotions, which lie between winning and losing, jubilation and woe, brilliant victory and bitter defeat.
One way or another, both would have been possible for the BMW WilliamsF1 Team at the final race in Suzuka. The fight

was for the most important title that an automobile manufacturer as well as a Formula One team involved in international motor sport can achieve – the FIA Formula One Constructors' title. The positions were amazingly close with Ferrari having 147 points and the BMW WilliamsF1 Team 144 points.

Following the final qualifying on Saturday and the confusion caused by the rain, it was clear in the BMW WilliamsF1 Team compound that this would be no easy race. One car on the front row and the other on the last row of the grid – it may have the appeal of being an extremely rare situation, but it was by no means what is wanted for a race which will decide the outcome of the championship.

Patrick Head, Technical Director at WilliamsF1, soon resorted to his characteristic English sense of humour. Bursting onto the scene of Ralf Schumacher's press conference, he took to the floor and said to the assembled journalists, "Ralf is looking forward to starting from the very back. It makes a race all the more interesting." Ralf responded to Patrick's statement: "I just said the exact same thing, Patrick."

Only 24 hours later, everything has been decided. Montoya, initially leading the race, dropped out due to a technical failure. Following a race full of challenges and drama, as well as his own mistakes, Ralf Schumacher finished in twelfth place and without a single point.

Still bearing the fresh disappointment of a completely unsatisfactory race, Ralf Schumacher said, "We messed several things up at the end of the season. We could have come away with the Drivers' Championship and the Constructors' Championship, but we lost both opportunities." His team mate Montoya, on the other hand, found some words of racing philosophy, "That's racing. You have to be able to deal with it. You win and you lose."

Theissen, highly thought of in the drivers' enclosure for his clear statements, continued in the same vein, "For us, this race and the whole season was an emotional rollercoaster. A constant up and down. Our team still wasn't ready for the title. We made too many mistakes." Theissen's conclusion after 16 races in 14 countries was that, "The year had two aspects to it. It got off to a disappointing start. The new car was not as fast as we had hoped. However, we then began catching up with a vengeance. The team worked very well, with the WilliamsF1 engineers working particularly well on the aerodynamic side and on the chassis set-up. By the middle of the season, we were really able to catch up with the front-runners. There were moments during the second half of the season when we had the upper hand. After the race at Monaco, we began to notch up some extremely commendable results which suddenly set us amongst the elite – something completely unexpected at that point in time. We fought for the world championship title until the very last race. In the end, it was by far the most successful season that our team has enjoyed. Even last year, Ferrari had twice as many points as any other team – even twice as many as we did in second place. And if we are now at a stage where we are fighting it out down to the very last race, it shows that we have reached the level required to win a world championship. That makes me very confident about next year."

Prof Dr Burkhard Göschel, Member of the Board of Management of BMW AG, Development and Purchasing, insisted on being present at the final race to keep his fingers crossed for the team. He came with his heart fully committed to the matter, "I'm here as a Formula One enthusiast rather than as a board member."

His analysis of the season and the resulting measures which need to be taken shows that despite his passion for motor sport, he has not lost sight of what is technically required. Prof Göschel summarises, "The risk with a new car is that it won't work perfectly from the start and that we won't understand everything about it. It only makes clear that tremendous preparation and development is required in order to get a new car up and running. As engineers we know that there is no difference in this respect between Formula One and road car engineering."

One thing is certain, and that is the intensification of the collaboration between BMW and WilliamsF1, as Prof Göschel again emphasised in Suzuka, "We will work increasingly closer together on the development of the engine and entire car. Apart from developing and providing the engine, BMW will jointly work with WilliamsF1 in the areas of transmission and electronics. In addition, we will integrate the BMW know-how and resources into other areas, such as aerodynamics, for example. In order to realise this, we will introduce joint project management with integrated processes. We will put together mixed teams for specific tasks to ensure that the integration of BMW and WilliamsF1 really takes place. This means that BMW and WilliamsF1 will work together a lot more closely than has been the case in the past. Once our agreement had been signed, the conditions were created for this to succeed."

As BMW Motorsport Director Dr Theissen points out, being "runner-up" in 2003 was a "tremendous step forward". The BMW WilliamsF1 Team was the only racing team able to celebrate one-two victories in the 2003 season and the BMW WilliamsF1 Team fought hard to earn 52 more points than they accumulated in the previous season. With four victories, they have three more than in the previous year. Moreover, the BMW WilliamsF1 Team leads with regard to reliability statistics, as no team completed more race laps than the BMW WilliamsF1 Team (1,800).

Prof Göschel adds, "The team has caught up with the top team in Formula One in 2003. With this technical competence and the experience from the past, the BMW WilliamsF1 Team has the best basis for the 2004 season." Regardless of whether it will be 16, 17 or even 18 races, the 2004 season will be long and hard, bristling with gripping duels, fascinating technology and human dramas. It will provide a fitting occasion to once again have a proper, exuberant party after the final race, with lots of singing and perhaps again with "Smoke on the Water" by Deep Purple and "Ticket to Ride" by the Beatles. And maybe there will even be an encore from Queen for the BMW WilliamsF1 Team and the two lightning fast, singing lads. Maybe "We are the Champions"...

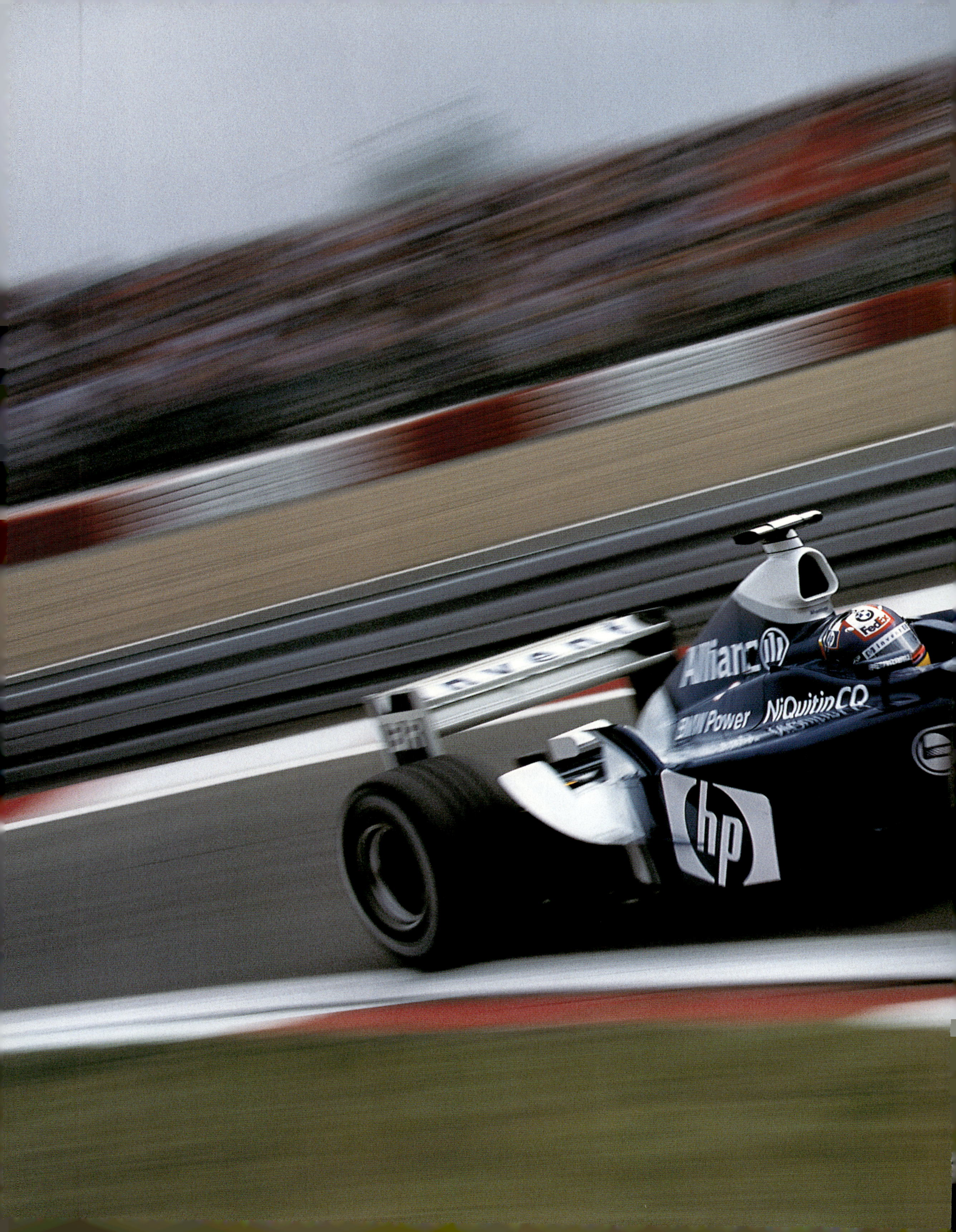
NiQuitin CQ
Power
hp

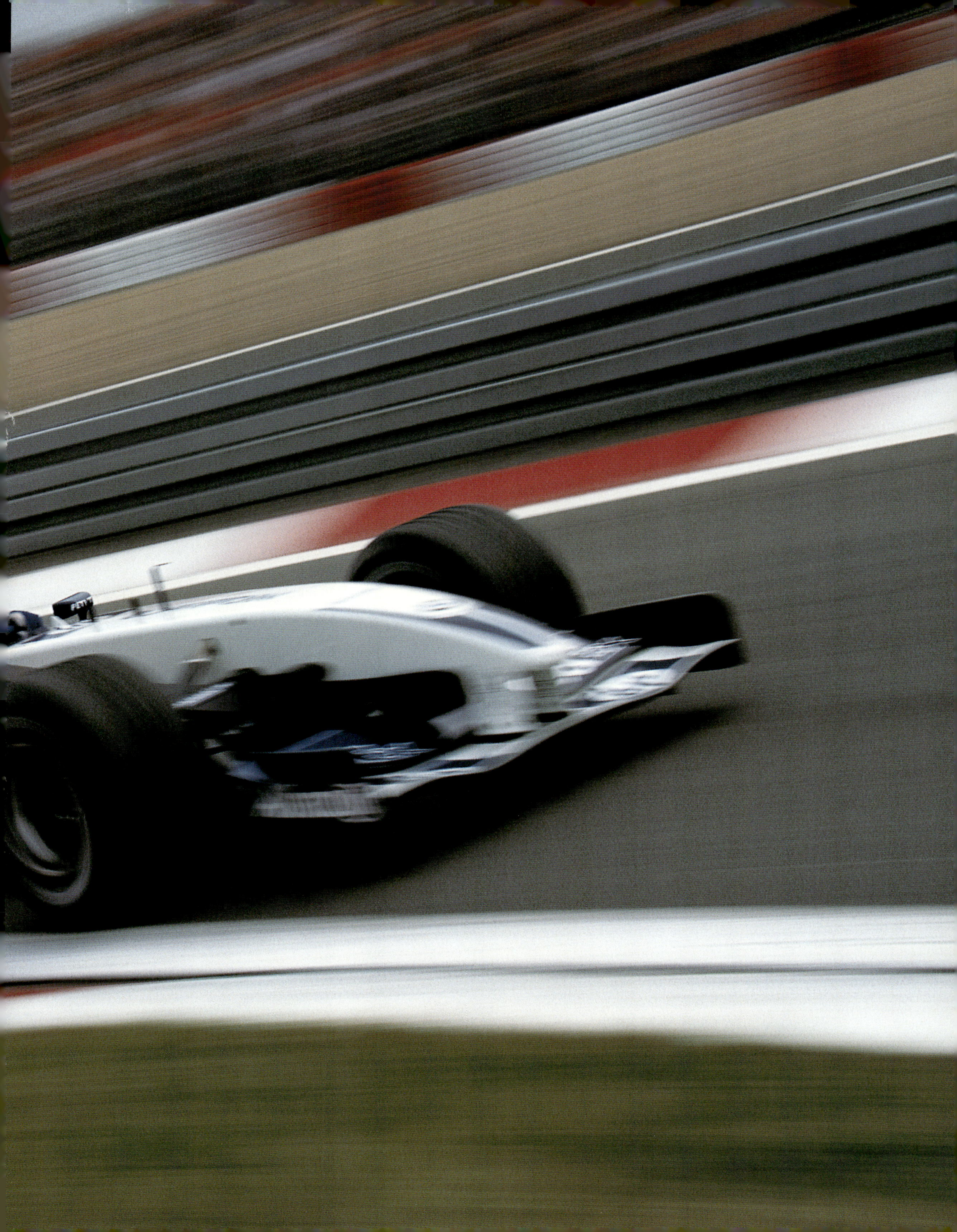

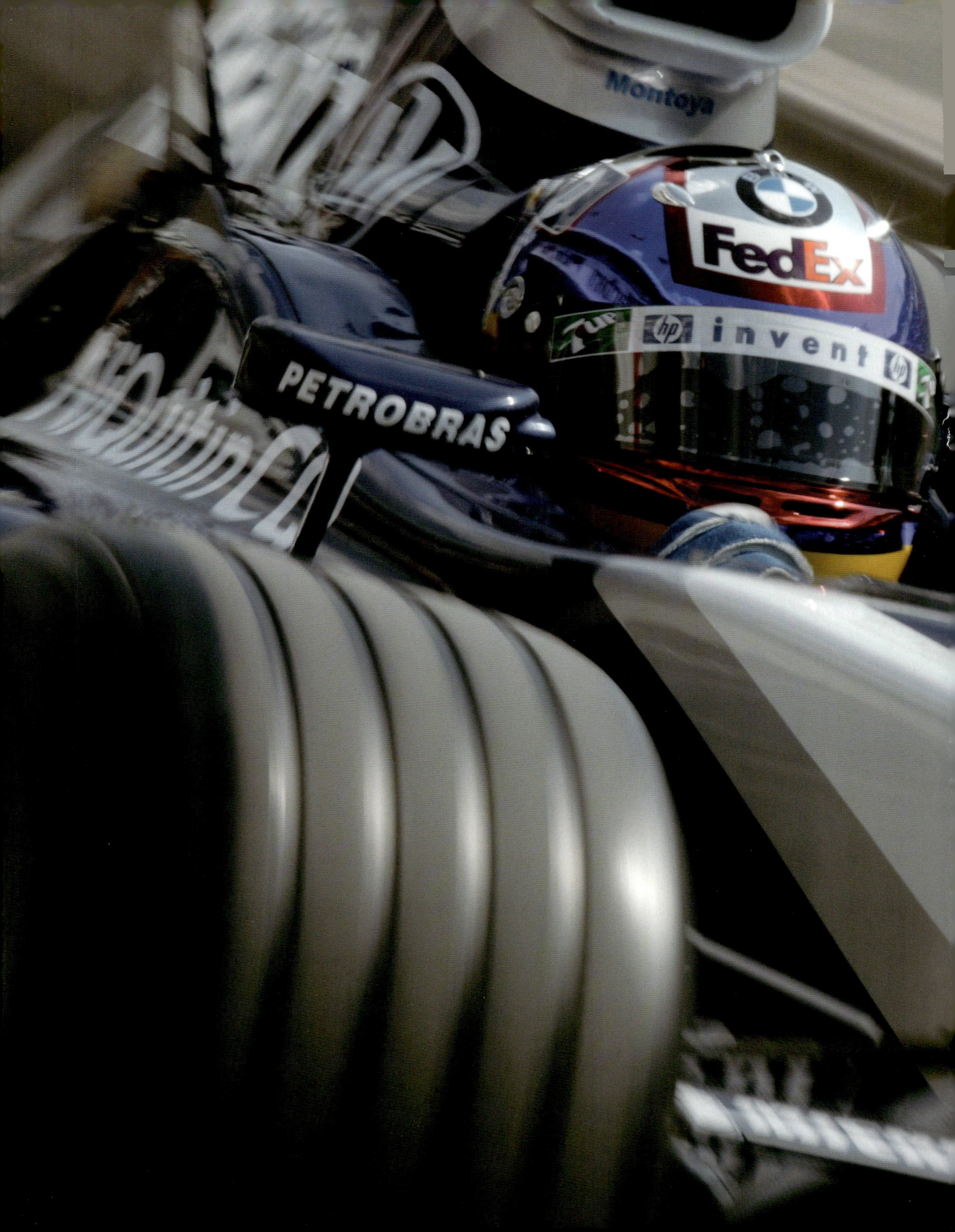
Montoya
FedEx
hp invent hp
PETROBRAS

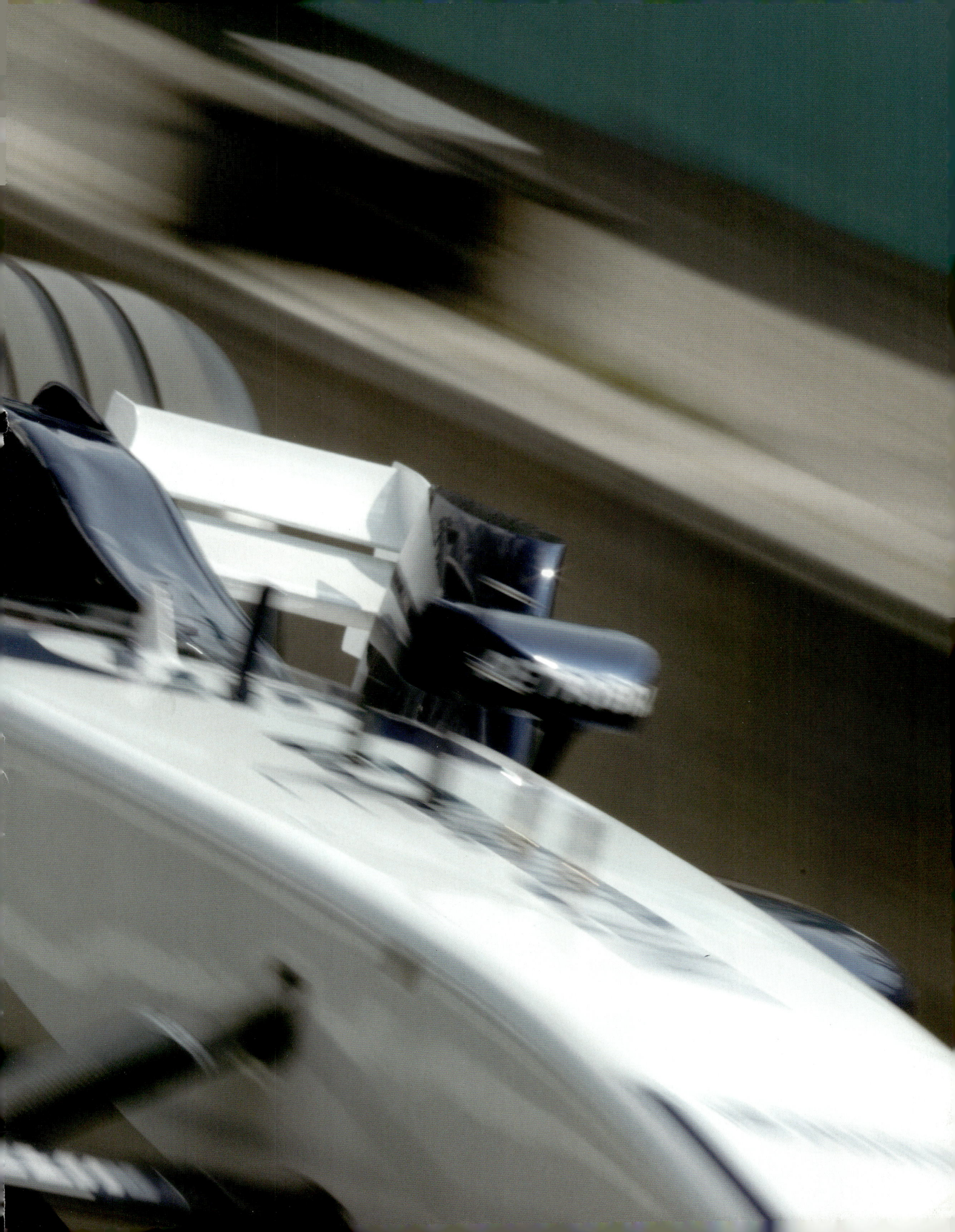

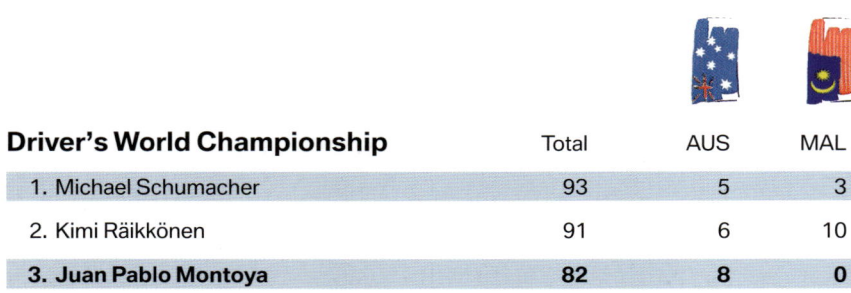

Driver's World Championship	Total	AUS	MAL	BRA	SMR	ESP
1. Michael Schumacher	93	5	3	-	10	10
2. Kimi Räikkönen	91	6	10	8	8	-
3. Juan Pablo Montoya	**82**	**8**	**0**	**-**	**2**	**5**
4. Rubens Barrichello	65	-	8	-	6	6
5. Ralf Schumacher	**58**	**1**	**5**	**2**	**5**	**4**
6. Fernando Alonso	55	2	6	6	3	8
7. David Coulthard	51	10	-	5	4	-
8. Jarno Trulli	33	4	4	1	0	-
9. Jenson Button	17	0	2	-	1	0
10. Mark Webber	17	-	-	0	-	2
11. Heinz-Harald Frentzen	13	3	0	4	0	-
12. Giancarlo Fisichella	12	0	-	10	0	-
13. Cristiano da Matta	10	-	0	0	0	3
14. Nick Heidfeld	6	-	1	-	0	0
15. Olivier Panis	6	-	-	-	0	-
16. Jacques Villeneuve	6	0	-	3	-	-
17. Marc Gené	**4**					
18. Takuma Sato	3					
19. Ralph Firman	1	-	0	-	-	1
20. Justin Wilson	1	-	-	-	-	0
21. Antonio Pizzonia	0	0	-	-	0	-
22. Jos Verstappen	0	0	0	-	-	0
23. Nicolas Kiesa	0					
24. Zsolt Baumgartner	0					

Constructors' World Championship	Total	AUS	MAL	BRA	SMR	ESP
1. Scuderia Ferrari Marlboro	158	5	11	0	16	16
2. BMW WilliamsF1 Team	**144**	**9**	**5**	**2**	**7**	**9**
3. West McLaren Mercedes	142	16	10	13	12	0
4. Mild Seven Renault F1 Team	88	6	10	7	3	8
5. Lucky Strike BAR Honda	26	0	2	3	1	0
6. Sauber Petronas	19	3	1	4	0	0
7. Jaguar Racing	18	0	0	0	0	2
8. Panasonic Toyota Racing	16	0	0	0	0	3
9. Jordan Ford	13	0	0	10	0	1
10. European Minardi Cosworth	0	0	0	0	0	0

Legend: 0 = Finished outside points   - = Retired   no insert = did not compete

Statistics Season 2003

AUT	MCO	CDN	EUR	FRA	GBR	DEU	HUN	ITA	USA	JPN
10	6	10	4	6	5	2	1	10	10	1
8	8	3	-	5	6	-	8	5	8	8
-	**10**	**6**	**8**	**8**	**8**	**10**	**6**	**8**	**3**	**-**
6	1	4	6	2	10	-	-	6	-	10
3	**5**	**8**	**10**	**10**	**0**	**-**	**5**	**-**	**-**	**0**
-	4	5	5	-	-	5	10	1	-	-
4	2	-	0	4	4	8	4	-	-	6
1	3	-	-	-	3	6	2	-	5	4
5	-	-	2	-	1	1	0	-	-	5
2	-	2	3	3	0	0	3	2	-	0
-	-	-	0	0	0	-	-	0	6	-
-	0	-	0	-	-	0	-	0	2	-
0	0	0	-	0	2	3	0	-	0	2
-	0	-	1	0	0	0	0	0	4	0
-	0	1	-	1	0	4	-	-	-	0
0	-	-	-	0	0	0	-	3	-	
								4		
										3
0	0	-	0	0	0	-			-	0
0	-	-	0	0	0	-	-	-	1	0
0	-	0	0	0	-					
-	-	0	0	0	0	-	0	-	0	0
						0	0	0	0	0
									-	0
16	7	14	10	8	15	2	1	16	10	11
3	**15**	**14**	**18**	**18**	**8**	**10**	**11**	**12**	**3**	**0**
12	10	3	0	9	10	8	12	5	8	14
1	7	5	5	0	3	11	12	1	5	4
5	0	0	2	0	1	1	0	3	0	8
0	0	0	1	0	0	0	0	0	10	0
2	0	2	3	3	0	0	3	2	1	0
0	0	1	0	1	2	7	0	0	0	2
0	0	0	0	0	0	0	0	0	2	0
0	0	0	0	0	0	0	0	0	0	0

Publisher: BMW AG, München 2003

Copyright for this issue: Egmont vgs verlagsgesellschaft mbH, Köln 2003

Author: Christoph Schulte

Photography: Bildagentur Kräling, Andreas Beil, Rainer Schlegelmilch, Daniel Reinhard, Florian Jaenicke, Jürgen Skarwan

Type setting: Achim Münster, Overath

Lithography: Medien Team-Vreden, Vreden

Printing: Appl, Wemding

© 2003 BMW AG, D-80788 München

All rights reserved.

No part of this publication may be reproduced, stored in a retrieval system or transmitted, in any form or by any means, electronic, mechanical, photocopying, recording or otherwise, without prior permission in writing from BMW AG.

ISBN 3-8025-1587-0